The Real School Safety Problem

The Real School Safety Problem

THE LONG-TERM CONSEQUENCES OF HARSH SCHOOL PUNISHMENT

Aaron Kupchik

UNIVERSITY OF CALIFORNIA PRESS

University of California Press, one of the most distinguished university presses in the United States, enriches lives around the world by advancing scholarship in the humanities, social sciences, and natural sciences. Its activities are supported by the UC Press Foundation and by philanthropic contributions from individuals and institutions. For more information, visit www.ucpress.edu.

University of California Press
Oakland, California

Library of Congress Cataloging-in-Publication Data

Names: Kupchik, Aaron, author.
Title: The real school safety problem : the long-term consequences of
   harsh school punishment / Aaron Kupchik.
Description: Oakland, California : University of California Press, [2016]
   | "2016 | Includes bibliographical references and index.
Identifiers: LCCN 2015050882 (print) | LCCN 2016000504 (ebook) |
   ISBN 9780520284197 (cloth : alk. paper) | ISBN 9780520284203
   (pbk. : alk. paper) | ISBN 9780520959842 (ebook)
Subjects: LCSH: Schools—Security measures—United States. | School
   violence—United States—Prevention. | Discipline of children—United
   States—Psychological aspects.
Classification: LCC LB2866 .K86 2016 (print) | LCC LB2866 (ebook) |
   DDC 371.70973—dc23
LC record available at http://lccn.loc.gov/2015050882

Manufactured in the United States of America

25 24 23 22 21 20 19 18 17 16
10 9 8 7 6 5 4 3 2 1

This book is dedicated to my parents, I. Leona and Herbert Z Kupchik

Contents

Illustrations

TABLES

Acknowledgments

There should be few things more joyful than writing the acknowledgments to one's book. The fact that I'm writing this means that my book is finished and going to press, and it's an opportunity to reflect on how lucky I am that I have so much support from colleagues, friends, and family. And yet it's difficult, mostly because I'm afraid that I'll leave some people out. If that's you, please forgive my oversight.

To start, I want to thank my wife, Elena, and my kids, Sarah and Alexis. I am lucky to have a family that supports my career and allows me the time to devote to research, writing, travel to conferences, and other benefits of academic life. They are very patient, always willing to listen when I am excited about my work, and there to pick me up when I get depressed about how much we do wrong when it comes to school punishment and security. I also want to thank my parents, to whom this book is dedicated. Every year, as my children grow and I learn more about the challenges and joys of parenting, it becomes clearer to me how much my parents have done and how privileged I have been to have them to guide and support me.

I am also fortunate to work in a department where I feel appreciated, and I am grateful for all my colleagues in the Department of Sociology and Criminal Justice at the University of Delaware, who help make it a collaborative and collegial workplace where scholarship and teaching are valued. Thanks in particular to Kirk Williams, my department chair, for his support; and to the Department Policy Committee, who agreed to fund my research in Alabama. I also have colleagues with whom I can share ideas and from whom I always learn. I greatly appreciate the exchange of ideas I receive from Ronet Bachman, Joel Best, Anne Bowler, John Brent, Aaron Fichtelberg, Ben Fleury-Steiner, Santhi Leon, Susan Miller, Tom Mowen, and Yasser Payne, among others.

I have learned a great deal from colleagues and friends in the broader academic and child advocacy communities, and I continue to learn from such bright and passionate people. I appreciate the guidance on this project I received from Tom Catlaw, Jeff Fagan, Katie Farina, Dorrell Green, David Greenberg, Paul Hirschfield, Chandlee Kuhn, Akiva Liberman, Malik Muhammad, Anthony Peguero, Brad Snyder, Geoff Ward, and Franklin Zimring. I am also grateful for the insightful perspectives on my draft manuscript from Allison Ann Payne, Anthony Peguero, and Geoff Ward.

The University of California Press has been a delight to work with as well. I want to thank Maura Roessner for her guidance from the start of this project, and Jack Young for his help along the way. It has been a pleasure working with Richard Earles, who copyedited the manuscript, and Jessica Moll, who oversaw its production.

The staff at the Southern Poverty Law Center in Alabama was so gracious and generous in facilitating my research. I appreciate everything done for me by Nanyamka Shukura, Jadine Johnson, Ebony Glenn-Howard, and Maria Morris. Last but not least, I want to thank the families in Mobile, Alabama, who gave me their time and shared their stories with me. The interviews that I describe in chapter 3, and that are central to much of what I discuss in this book, were at times very difficult to conduct. Listening to parents talk about their frustration, anger, and shame at how their children were being mistreated by schools—the institution that is supposed to be dedicated to their learning and welfare—was not easy. I imagine it was infinitely more difficult for them to share their pain with me. Hopefully, as we learn more and think more about school punishment and security, fewer parents and children will have to go through such battles.

1 Introduction

Schools across the United States are in a school safety crisis. But it's not the one that most might imagine it to be. The crisis is *not* that our schools arc at risk of another mass shooting like those at Columbine or Sandy Hook. And it's *not* that children are out of control, with violence and theft rampant in schools. Such situations are horrifying (particularly mass shootings) and devastating, and we ought to do what we can to prevent them. But they do not exist at crisis levels. The crisis—the real school safety problem—is that we have implemented a series of practices that go too far in promoting school security and punishment, and as a result do considerable harm to students, schools, families, and communities.

Parents, school officials, and policy-makers often ask the wrong questions. For example, consider my seven-year-old daughter's reaction when I told her about the 2012 shootings at Sandy Hook Elementary School in Newtown, Connecticut. I expected a ten-minute conversation, in which I would tell her, she would be scared, and I would comfort her. I was so wrong. We talked for well over an hour. She was calm and curious, not scared. She asked me question after question about what had happened. At first she wanted to know the specifics of the event itself, in an attempt to wrap her mind around how such tragedy is possible: Were the children who died all in one classroom, or in many? Did they die right away? Did the killer use several guns, or reload one? And so on. But then her questions shifted to trying to come to grips with how the tragedy could have been prevented, what her school does to prevent violence, and what schools *should* do. She wanted to know what was done to diagnose and treat gunman Adam Lanza's mental health issues, whether the door to the school was locked, how Lanza was able to enter the school, whether they should have had a police officer there, and whether police officers should be at schools everywhere. She wanted to know whether schools were safe, and what we could best do to keep schools safe.

Thankfully, I felt pretty confident in answering her questions, since I'd spent the past several years trying to understand what schools do to keep kids safe, how well these practices work, and what effects they have. But it occurred to me how few people ask these questions that are apparent to a seven-year-old. Instead of *asking* whether tighter security and harsher punishments are a good idea for schools, the public, school administrators, politicians, and others simply *assume* that they are. Rather than engaging with the problem of school safety and seeking information, as my daughter did, these groups more often respond out of fear. As a result, their assumptions about security and punishment are usually wrong because they misunderstand the real problem with school safety. The problem is *not* that students misbehave too much, that school gates aren't sufficiently secure, or that we don't have enough surveillance over our kids. Instead, the real problems with school safety are the well-intended but misguided policies we have put in place over the past twenty years. Our fears about school safety have caused us to alter public education in a way that has hurt children more than it might help them.

Consider the response to the horrible events at Newtown. Soon after the massacre, the National Rifle Association (NRA) made headlines by proposing that all schools in the United States hire armed guards. The public response to their suggestion was harsh, with politicians and advocates calling it absurd (among other things). While I agree with the critics that it was a bad idea, the backlash against it was political hypocrisy, seeing as how it isn't too far from what we currently do. For example, then New York City Council Speaker (and 2013 mayoral candidate) Christine Quinn called the NRA's proposal "Some of the most stupid, asinine, insensitive, ridiculous comments I have ever heard in the public arena."[1] New York City

Mayor Michael Bloomberg called the NRA's proposal "a paranoid, dystopian vision of a more dangerous and violent America where everyone is armed and no place is safe."[2] And yet, during Bloomberg's time as mayor, the New York City Police Department (NYPD) had a School Safety Division of over five thousand school safety officers policing the city's public schools. Their job requirements are less strict than those for other NYPD officers, and they receive less training and pay than other officers. And while they do not carry guns, they do have arrest powers and are backed up by police officers who are armed. New York City was sued by the American Civil Liberties Union and the New York Civil Liberties Union because of alleged unfair treatment of students,[3] and several investigations have documented abusive treatment at the hands of these officers.[4] Is that really so different from what the NRA proposed? Don't hold me to this, but I think the NRA's proposal may be better than what went on in New York City public schools during the Bloomberg administration.

The NRA wasn't the only group offering more security as a solution, either. Senator Barbara Boxer (D–CA) proposed stationing National Guard troops in schools across the country. Ironically, Mayor Bloomberg, who oversaw NYPD's massive School Safety Division, called Senator Boxer's plan "ridiculous," stating that "You can't live your life that way. You'd be in a prison."[5] President Obama's January 2013 executive order in response to Newtown also proposed more policing in schools. While the gun control measures in this order drew the most attention by far, it also included more funding for police officers in schools.

We have already been fortifying schools for the past twenty years. We have added police officers, surveillance cameras, and locked gates. We now have drug-sniffing police dogs searching students' possessions. We follow zero-tolerance policies and suspend, expel, or arrest students for minor misbehavior that would only have led to a trip to the principal's office a generation ago. And so on. Each of these reforms is justified as a means to maintain safety: metal detectors are intended to prevent guns from entering the school, dogs to detect and eliminate drugs from the school, and zero-tolerance policies to target students who are violent and remove them from school before they can hurt other children. Of course, the causes of these practices are more complex and involve racial and class tensions, as well as insecurity about schools more generally.[6] But they promise to maintain safety by securing the school's borders, policing students within the school, and punishing students who are seen as potential threats.

Over the past twenty years, while we have been punishing students in increasingly harsh ways and making schools look more like prisons, our policy-makers have failed to ask the questions my daughter raised. Those who study school security and school discipline have been warning that these practices are ineffective and often harmful. Yet the public, policy-makers, and school officials either haven't been listening or don't care whether these practices are effective. They meet political needs, demonstrating that politicians and school administrators are taking action to protect children. The assumption that more invasive security and harsher punishments mean less trouble, less disorder, less danger, and more safety has either caused or allowed schools across the country to beef up security and punishments. Our children pay for the fact that adults misunderstand what the real problem with school safety is.

Certainly, horrific events like the shooting at Newtown are very important and offer many lessons. But they are rare. The horror at Newtown does not define the danger that students across the United States face on a daily basis. This danger—the real school safety problem—is the policies that we have put in place to try to keep children safe in schools. These policies, which have us guard the gates of schools, police their interiors, and respond vigorously to any disorder, are the real problem because they are mostly ineffective, while causing harm to students, schools, families, and communities. Perhaps it shouldn't be surprising that our school safety practices are often ineffective and even harmful to children, since we have made massive changes to schools that are guided by assumptions rather than evidence. But it is wrong to subject our kids to harm based on excessive devotion to security and punishment strategies in schools. The point of this book is to help improve this state of affairs, to discuss what we know about effective school security and punishment in the hope of advancing a real dialogue about the issue.

OVERREACTING TO OUR FEARS

Imagine that school crime has been decreasing for over twenty years, nationwide. Imagine kids in school today reporting that they are injured less, get in fewer fights, are less likely to carry a weapon to school, and less likely to have something stolen, compared to kids in the early 1990s. Imagine that school is one of the safest places for kids to be, that they are far more likely to be killed at home by a parent or other caregiver, to drown, or to die in a fire, for example, than to be killed at school.

All of this is actually true. Schools are safer, and students better behaved (in terms of fighting, stealing, weapon carrying, etc.) than they were in the early 1990s, when the Department of Education began collecting annual nationwide data on school crime. And yet parents' fears about the dangers kids face at school are high. In a 2013 Gallup poll, 33 percent of parents with a child in kindergarten to twelfth grade stated that they feared for his or her physical safety while at school, even though only 10 percent of these same parents stated that their children had voiced any concern about their own safety.[7] This fear among parents and other adults[8] is a significant problem, because it has caused us to change how we run schools. Over the past twenty years we have put police officers and other security guards in schools, posted surveillance cameras, and installed metal detectors. The criminal justice system is now a real part of our educational system. This doesn't just happen in inner-city schools with mostly students of color and low-income children, but in wealthy communities with mostly White students, too.[9] In order to keep students in line we have beefed up punishments within school so that minor misbehavior—talking back to teachers, cursing, and other types of typical adolescent shenanigans—now results in suspension. We use police dogs to search our children's belongings—not just in response to an incident, but as a matter of course. Either we don't care whether these practices actually work to keep kids safe or we've just assumed they will, without bothering to consider any evidence on whether or not they work. The evidence that is available tells us that our efforts have been misguided—an overreaction that hurts kids.

Consider, for example, the use of a chemical spray—a version of mace, or pepper spray, called "Freeze +P"—in Birmingham, Alabama, public schools. Students working with the Southern Poverty Law Center recently won a lawsuit against police officers stationed in schools; the students sued the police for repeatedly using mace on students, even when there was no immediate danger to anyone. Students named in the lawsuit claim that they have been sprayed for watching—not participating in, but just watching—

fights in the hallways, for running on school grounds, and even while already restrained by other security guards or police. One complainant, K. B., was four months pregnant when she was involved in a macing incident. According to her, she was upset after being sexually harassed (being called a "ho" and other offensive terms) by another student, so she walked away to her next class, crying. When a police officer approached her and she failed to "calm down" as ordered, the officer sprayed her in the face.[10]

Certainly, police officers should have authority to use force if it is necessary to protect themselves or others from a real threat of serious violence. But cases described in the lawsuit included no threat of violence to the officers, and rarely to other students (if there was a threat, it was in the form of a fistfight, not a deadly weapon). Instead the case demonstrates what happens when an entire student body is perceived as threatening and in need of aggressive policing. Birmingham schools tend to be overcrowded and disorderly, and they are overwhelmingly composed of low-income Black students. Many police might fear these students, seeing them as potential criminals.[11] It's a shame that fear causes adults to see a child as a criminal who requires force, not as a teenager struggling to cope with real-life problems (as in the case of K. B.). In such a case, fear is dehumanizing—it leads adults to see kids only as threats, not as children who need care or young people learning to be citizens. Harsh, abusive actions like this can seem reasonable only if the public has blind faith in rigid security measures.

Although this example offers a good illustration of how fear of school violence can lead us to bad policy choices, it's also a little misleading because it's such an extreme case. A majority of high schools across the country have police officers in them, but such brutality is exceptionally rare. Moreover, police in schools do many good things for children. They mentor students and serve as positive role models, and they are there to protect and restore order in case real crime occurs on campus. This is all true and is too often dismissed by advocates for removing police from schools.

Yet there is a growing body of research showing that on the balance, the daily presence of police can do more harm than good. Certainly they are needed in some schools with real violence problems. Thankfully, though, most schools are relatively peaceful, with only occasional fights—fewer than they had a generation ago, when teachers and administrators were able to break them up without police intervention. The harm comes because the presence of police officers changes the school environment in subtle but important ways. Schools shift from sites of caring, where students' academic and social needs are met, to sites of law enforcement, with a greater focus on crimes and legal responses to student problems than on students' academic, social, and emotional needs.

Recently, in October 2015, we saw another example of harm at the hands of a school police officer when Richland County, South Carolina, Sheriff's Deputy Ben Fields was captured on camera throwing a female student to the ground and across a classroom. Mr. Fields was fired within days of the incident, as the cell phone footage went viral, being reported by major news media and social media as well. The fact that Fields was fired shows that the Sheriff's Department recognized that his actions were inconsistent with department policy and procedure. But if we look more carefully at this incident, it highlights other potential problems with school policing that go well beyond a single officer's violent overreaction. One issue is that an officer was called to the classroom because the student would not follow an order to leave the room—she was banished from the classroom for having her cell phone out, despite the fact that she put it away when asked and apologized to the teacher. A second issue is that the child who stood her ground and refused to leave her seat was in foster care.[12] These two aspects of the incident are important, because they demonstrate some of the hazards of putting officers in schools across the country: (1) officers are asked to respond to behavior that is against school rules, but illegal only under a very loose interpretation of criminal law; and (2) they are asked to respond to the actions of students whose complicated lives and histories they have no way of knowing about, but whose trauma might be directing their behaviors.

In my book *Homeroom Security,* I reported the results of a multiyear study in which I shadowed police in schools. I was impressed with how much these officers, usually called "school resource officers" (SROs), cared for the children in their charge. They tried to mentor and teach them, and they were indeed positive role models. But at the same time, SROs are limited in their ability to truly help most kids. Often they are unable to hold their confidence and are insufficiently trained in how to respond to typical adolescent problems. They are excellent at responding to conflict, but typically with a rougher edge than someone who is instead trained in child development. While I never saw a student thrown across a room, I can understand how this might happen if an officer trained in responding to violence overreacts, without any consideration for why a student might refuse to leave her classroom (in the case of the South Carolina student, one might wonder whether her experience in foster care makes her less willing to relinquish control when she thinks she's being treated unfairly).

Of course, much of the current debate about school safety is framed by the goal of protecting schools from armed attackers, not policing young threats within the school. The truth is that we don't know whether more police in schools might prevent another Newtown. Events like that one— or the tragedy at Columbine High School in Colorado, which was both an armed attack and a crime committed by students—are so rare that it is difficult to know whether one or two officers per school might have an effect. One can look at Newtown, an elementary school without an SRO, and say that an officer or other armed guard might have prevented it. But what about Columbine, which had an SRO on campus at the time of the attack there? If we assume that a police officer on campus would have prevented the Newtown attack, wouldn't the same brand of logic have told us, based on the inability of an SRO's presence to prevent the tragedy at Columbine, that police presence doesn't prevent these types of horrific events? Research on whether the presence of SROs can make schools safer from more minor crimes suggests that it does not (I discuss this further in chapter 2).

Attempts to prevent school shootings by hiring more guards and SROs are a lot like the war on terror. In both scenarios, we are afraid and respond to this fear by trading something important for perceived security. In general, many Americans haven't cared much about the privacy they sacrifice in the name of security, but with Edward Snowden's revelations about the National Security Agency illegally spying on citizens, more Americans began to take note. In the war on terror, we sacrifice privacy for security (experts may debate whether actual security is achieved, but that is a debate for someone else to take up). When it comes to armed school guards, SROs, and increased punishments for student misbehavior, we make a parallel choice to sacrifice for the sake of security. Yet public and political rhetoric underestimate what we sacrifice and overestimate what we gain. In this book, I clarify the trade-off: What do we sacrifice when we ramp up school security and punishment efforts, and what do we gain?

CURRENT STATE OF AFFAIRS

The National Center for Education Statistics, a branch of the U.S. Department of Education, collects data every year on school crime and school security. In its annual report, "Indicators of School Crime and Safety," the center presents these data, including national trends on crime in schools (kindergarten through high school) since 1992. Figure 1 shows the most recent trend data available, clearly documenting the extraordinary decline in student victimization over the past twenty years.[13] These data come from surveys of youths in which they were asked whether they had been victims of crime over the past year, an extension (via the "School Crime Supplement") to the well-respected National Criminal Victimization Survey. While no survey data are perfect, there is no reason to think that errors in reporting would be greater today than they were in 1992, which means we can have confidence in the conclusion that schools across the country are safer, overall, than they were in the early 1990s.

Other sources of data confirm that schools have been getting safer. For example, the Youth Risk Behavior Survey, another well-respected, nationally representative data-collection effort, finds substantial declines in students' reports of whether they have been in a fight at school, or carried a weapon at school, between 1993 and 2013.[14]

Since I began my discussion with Newtown, though, I should also focus on fear of kids dying, not just concerns that they get beat up or stolen from. Figure 2 shows the number of homicides of students ages five to eighteen at school each year, which has also declined over the past twenty years.[15] The decline in figure 2 is much less stark, and less consistent, that that in figure 1, but this makes sense given that student deaths were so rare to begin with. Unlike figure 1, which lets us conclude that schools are safer places than they were twenty years ago, figure 2 tells us that deaths at school have always been rare. To put it into perspective, there were more than twice as many infants who died from whooping cough (twenty-five) or syphilis (twenty-eight) in 2010 than there were children who

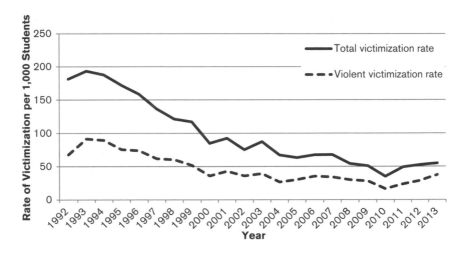

Figure 1. Total and violent victimization rates per 1,000 students, ages twelve to eighteen, 1992–2013. Source: table 2.1 in Simone Robers et al. (2015) "Indicators of school crime and safety: 2014." Washington, DC: National Center for Education Statistics, U.S. Department of Education.

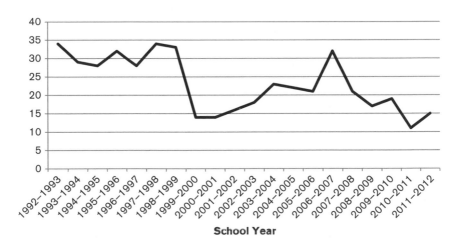

Figure 2. Numbers of homicides of youths ages five to eighteen at school, 1992–2012. Source: figure 1.1 in Simone Robers et al. (2015) "Indicators of school crime and safety: 2014." Washington, DC: National Center for Education Statistics, U.S. Department of Education.

suffered violent deaths at school during the 2010–11 school year; there were 129 times more deaths of children ages fourteen or younger in motor vehicle accidents (1,418) than there were students of any age who died in schools that year.[16]

If we look at other data that describe youths' lives more broadly, we see additional support for the overall message conveyed by these school surveys. According to the Centers for Disease Control and Prevention, teenage pregnancy is less common now than twenty years ago, age at first sexual activity has increased, and alcohol use and most forms of drug use by adolescents are declining.[17] And it's well documented that juvenile crime is much lower, generally, than it was during its peak in the early 1990s. There are a lot of reasons to be very confident that kids today are, overall, better behaved than kids twenty years ago.

The data are clear and convincing that schools are safer, nationally. Yet since these are national-level data, they may hide the fact that some schools have gotten worse. Certainly, there are some pockets of crime, some schools in which violence has escalated and continues to get worse. These schools are important and require intervention—but they are exceptions and should not be used to set the tone for national school policy debates. Unfortunately, though, that is precisely what has happened. We hear about those rare schools with increasing problems or isolated cases of school violence—or worse, as in the case of mass tragedies such as those at Columbine and Sandy Hook—and we assume that students are simultaneously out of control and in danger.

Our response has been to pursue two related strategies: (1) to protect the borders of schools in an effort to keep out any threats; and (2) to police and punish students more rigorously, so as to weed out those who may harm others. Some school practices are clearly intended to do only one of these two functions. One example is the use of locked doors, clearly intended to prevent intruders from accessing the school. Another is the increased use of suspension as a method of removing kids believed to be negative influences and/or potential threats. Indeed numbers of student suspensions have risen, going from 1.7 million in 1974 (3.7 percent of the student population) to 3.3 million (6.9 percent) in 2006. In the 2009–10 school year, more than 2,600 high schools in the nation suspended over 25 percent of their student bodies at least once.[18] In my research I've found that suspension is commonly used for very minor offenses, typically in response to behaviors such as talking back to teachers.

Other school strategies aim more broadly by trying to both secure the school's borders and police the students within. The best example of this is the use of SROs. Though practically unheard of twenty-five years ago, an armed police officer or security guard was present in 63 percent of high schools during 2009–10, according to the National Center for Education Statistics.[19] Police, security, and other law enforcement do many things at once. They mentor students, they teach law-related classes, they are first-responders in case of crisis, and they respond to more mundane crimes that occur on campus (e.g., drug or alcohol possession). Their presence is a key aspect of the changes that have occurred in schools, since they are one of the most visible features of the new school security regime.

In this book, I focus primarily on the second of these strategies—how we police and punish youths—rather than on how we secure schools' borders from outside threats, for a few important reasons. One is that I am most concerned with how we treat students, not how we treat visitors to the school. A second is that efforts to secure schools' borders are less contentious; while they may be expensive (a subject I discuss in chapter 7), there are few other documented harms that come from locked doors, cameras at the school's entrance, and visitor entrance policies. In contrast, the ways that we police and punish children in schools—particularly how we punish those who are seen as threats to the school—have many harms.

In sum, the current state of affairs is a curious one. Compared to a generation ago, school crime is down, schools are safe places for most youths, and students are better behaved, overall. And yet we behave as if the opposite were true—as if today's kids are menaces who need greater surveillance and restrictions and are in danger of ever-more-frequent attacks.

EXPLAINING SCHOOL SECURITY AND PUNISHMENT

When I talk about the problems with school security and punishment today, I'm almost always asked why we have the policies we do. I find it difficult to answer this in a straightforward way, because the answers commonly assumed to be true are simply not true. For example, the buildup of school security and punishment is most certainly not a response to high levels of student misbehavior—at least not in most schools, where student misbehavior and violence have been plummeting. Student crime may have been a reason why many such practices began in the early 1990s, but this cannot explain why schools have accelerated the buildup of school security and invested heavily in increasingly severe school punishments since then.

We also can't explain school security as a result of its effectiveness, as I discuss in greater detail in chapter 2. Generally, school crime and student misbehavior have been decreasing at the same time that school security and punishments have been increasing. But despite the timing of these events, there is no compelling evidence that increases in policing, surveillance, suspensions, and the like have made schools safer. It is certainly true that schools require strict disciplinary codes in order to best prevent student misbehavior—any parent should recognize the importance of clear, firm, and fairly enforced rules. But the changes over the past two decades aren't about strictness; they are about excluding youths from schools, arresting them for minor acts, and subjecting them to policing tactics not formerly seen in schools. Researchers have looked at whether the buildup of security and punishment seems to have caused decreasing crime or misbehavior rates, and no credible data have been able to show such a connection. In contrast, the evidence on effective school practices is very clear that one of the most effective ways to prevent school crime and student misbehavior is to have an inclusive school social climate.[20] As I discuss in chapter 2, this refers to a school environment where students feel respected, valued, listened to, and included in school governance; inclusive schools are ones that treat students like young citizens who are valued, not as potential threats. And yet research that examines how punishment and policing take shape in schools finds that we achieve exactly the opposite: that our security and punishment practices can alienate students from school, making them feel excluded and ignored.[21]

Another explanation often given for why we have so many police officers, surveillance cameras, drug-sniffing dogs, and suspensions in schools is that schools are responding to Columbine and other high-profile, terrifying incidents. I disagree with this as well. The changes to school punishment and security were already in progress prior to Columbine; in fact, Columbine had both surveillance cameras in use and an officer on staff. Columbine may have accelerated the trend, but it certainly did not create it.

Some, such as sociologist Richard Arum, have argued that contemporary school discipline is a response to a lack of legitimacy in school authority.[22] Arum begins his explanation with the civil rights era, in which several students challenged the constitutionality of school discipline, often when it was excessive or clearly racially motivated. Because many of these students won their lawsuits, Arum claims that this pro-student legal climate established the precedent of parents and students challenging the school's authority. This, he argues, continues today, as students and parents do not perceive the school's authority to be legitimate, meaning that they do not feel a moral obligation to abide by school rules; one result is that schools must do more to enforce these rules. But there are several flaws in Arum's argument. One is that even during what he calls the "pro-student legal era," schools still won most cases brought against them. Another is that after the early 1970s and the waning of the civil rights era, the percentage of court cases in which students were victorious against schools plummeted. A third is that it is entirely unclear how the correction of unjust and racist actions forty to fifty years ago translates into a perceived lack of legitimacy today. And finally, there is the fact that by today's standards (thankfully), we can see that schools were in the wrong and required legal intervention in order to correct unfair actions. Had they exercised fair authority to begin with, it is unlikely that so many legal cases would have been brought against them. Though it is indeed important for schools to be perceived as having moral authority, this is achieved through *fair* use of power, by listening to students, valuing them, and respecting them, not through denial of students' rights or oppressive discipline. A lack of legitimacy is therefore a consequence of school security and punishment, not a cause.

Other scholars rightly point toward the racially disproportionate use of school punishments and argue that racial animus is the cause of today's policies. It is absolutely true that youths of color are far more likely to be suspended, expelled, and arrested at school than are White youths; racialized perceptions of youths are central to the problem of school punishment, as I discuss in detail in chapter 3. And yet schools—particularly high schools—in communities all over the country have implemented rigid security and harsh punishment. Practices and policies vary in important ways that correspond to student race/ethnicity and poverty, and school security and punishment do indeed have graver and more frequent consequences for poor students and youths of color. But intense policing and harsh punishments are not just reserved for inner-city schools. Some similar practices are used in schools with mostly middle-class and White students, too. In other words, race and social class can explain a lot about school security and punishment, but this argument is incomplete, since it does not explain why schools hosting mostly middle-class White youths still rely on rigid policing, harsh punishment, and invasive surveillance. These practices may have begun as attempts to control poor youths and youths of color, but they have spread to schools—particularly high schools—across racial and class boundaries.[23]

So, what best explains the rampant spread of school security and punishment over the past generation? Fear and anxiety. We are afraid of, and anxious about, so many things; it goes well beyond our fear of student crime or armed attackers and includes the fear of incompetent teachers, of falling behind international educational standards, and other potential ills. Our fear and anxiety have two parallel effects. One is direct, in that we demand greater accountability for schools, more rules under which both students and teachers must operate, less authority for teachers to decide which students should avoid punishment, more police oversight, greater surveillance, and steeper penalties in case of misbehavior. The second is indirect: our anxieties ramp up the pressure put on schools (think standardized testing, Common Core Standards, Race to the Top, etc.). Schools respond by taking out their frustrations and difficulties on students, particularly the most frustrating students—those who misbehave or are just plain difficult to deal with. Like a parent who yells at her child after a horrible day in the office, so do teachers and administrators take out their frustrations on children. It's understandable, though it results in less empathy and patience for struggling students than typically caring and devoted educators might otherwise have.[24]

Furthermore, these fears and anxieties have come at a time when broader social currents direct them toward increased accountability and punishment. Contemporary society is often discussed as proceeding by a "neoliberal" logic, meaning that we are enthralled by corporate sensibilities of outsourcing, shifting accountability to lower levels (e.g., low-level employees lose their jobs before their bosses), rigid oversight, and benchmarks for productivity.[25] No Child Left Behind is the perfect illustration of this trend in schools, since it demands accountability for achievement as defined by standardized scores, and punishes schools that fail to meet their goals. A second important trend is mass incarceration, marked by fascination with the prison and a willingness to send more people there for longer sentences than ever before. The United States currently has the largest prison population and highest incarceration rate in the world, more than quadrupled since the 1970s.[26] We are a very punitive society—the most punitive among all industrialized nations. Given these two trends, and the fact that schools are under so much pressure because of the levels of anxiety and fear directed at them, it makes sense that the response is to impose more rules, harsher punishments, greater accountability for students, and more surveillance.

CHAPTER OUTLINE

In the following chapters I illustrate how the brand of school security and punishment that has spread across the country hurts kids. I begin in chapter 2 by discussing what we know about effective—and ineffective—school security and punishment practices. At this point, there is solid evidence that supports a number of promising programs; rather than treating students like threats or criminals, these programs treat them like valued children who make mistakes, and who need to learn from their mistakes. I also discuss the research that evaluates policing and punishment in schools; though there are some successes to report, the evidence tells us that our nationwide experiment in turning schools into fortresses hurts kids more than it helps them.

In chapter 3, I address the issue of racial disproportionality in school discipline and security. One of the most important harms—if not *the* most important—of excessive school security and punishment is that it increases inequality, particularly racial inequality. In this chapter, I discuss what we know about race and ethnicity, socioeconomic status, and other sources of inequality in society, and how they relate to school security and punishment.

Chapters 4 through 6 take a different approach, in two ways. One is that they present new evidence rather than summarizing and interpreting the existing research on school security and punishment. The second is that they consider how school security and punishment have farther-reaching, longer-lasting negative consequences than others have considered. By illustrating those consequences, these chapters demonstrate that the real problem with school security is the set of practices we have implemented across the country to keep schools safe. I focus heavily (but not only) on school suspension, since this is the most common way that schools respond to students who threaten the school's safety and order.

In chapter 4, coauthor Thomas Mowen and I share the experiences of parents and students we met in Mobile, Alabama, to illustrate that school punishment has broader consequences than have been considered before, as it can profoundly affect family life. Chapter 5 turns to another hot-button issue, bullying, as a way to demonstrate how harsh punishment and rigid security can have important negative effects on kids throughout schools, not just those who get in trouble. Here, Katie Farina and I discuss how unfair school rules and punishments might actually *increase* the chances that students are victims of bullying. In chapter 6, Thomas Catlaw and I look at long-term influences of schools' actions, and how school punishment can alienate students to the point where it inhibits voting and community volunteering years down the road, once students are adults in their late twenties.

I continue in chapter 7 by discussing the finances of school security and discipline. Everything has a cost—so how much does it cost us, in the short term and the long term, to police youths in schools and punish them the way we do? Current practices are profitable for private security companies eager to take ever larger portions of declining public dollars, but they are costly to everyone else.

Finally, in chapter 8, I conclude with principles for how schools can improve their efforts to keep children safe, while staying mindful of the potential obstacles that might prevent lasting improvements. There are several basic steps schools can take to improve safety while ensuring greater fairness—but the fact that schools' practices are now so well established means that real reform is a challenging task.

It's not easy to protect children in schools while punishing the ones who misbehave. Children can be very difficult to deal with, and teaching is

an extremely tough job—especially in today's climate of standardized testing and uncertain school funding. But the lack of public debate on the
topic is shameful and results in bad policies that hurt our kids. My hope is
that in the future, the public and policy-makers can have informed discussions in which we assess risks and benefits of actions in more thoughtful
and informed ways than we currently do. Our country needs to have a
more engaged, ongoing conversation about these issues, much like the
discussion I had with my daughter about Newtown.

2 Effective School Crime Prevention

In January 2013, I spoke at a U.S. House of Representatives Task Force Panel on youth violence. I discussed evidence on school violence prevention and focused, in particular, on how more policing and punishment are unlikely to help. After the panel, I was approached by a staff member of an organization that provides information to school administrators across the United States, who wanted to speak more about evidence regarding the effectiveness of policing in schools.[1] He told me that school administrators had been asking his association for advice on this topic in the aftermath of Newtown, and he was responsible for summarizing the research on it. We spoke briefly, and then continued our discussion via email. I summarized the research on this topic, noting that there is no credible statistical evidence that school resource officers (SROs) prevent crime on campus, and several qualitative studies that illustrate ways they can be harmful to students and school communities. In a response thanking me, he stated that

> The qualitative piece to me is really surprising and not compelling personally. I was arrested a few times as a juvenile and I never felt that the police in my schools had anything to do with that. I did not view them suspiciously and they did not make a difference in my academic or social experience in

school whatsoever. I certainly didn't like them, but the whole idea that they somehow make kids not want to come to school because they "fear" being arrested just doesn't ring true to me. If you have nothing to hide (and I never did anything on school premises that warranted an arrest), than there's nothing to worry about. I wonder if the sociocultural influence outside of school (how students whose parents or families have been mixed up with the law) makes them more freaked out by having law enforcement in school. If that's the case, then I still think that as long as you're not doing anything wrong at school, there's nothing to worry about.

What his email suggests to me is that he doesn't much care for the evidence because it doesn't match his individual experience or preconceived notions. I was taken aback by this resistance to evidence from someone who was responsible for doing research on the topic and helping advise school administrators across the nation.

Certainly, there are gaps in what we know about effective school safety practices, particularly when it comes to evidence about the effectiveness of police officers. But this doesn't mean that we know *nothing*, or that it is reasonable—particularly for someone in an advisory capacity who is assessing the research—to base professional judgment entirely on personal experiences. We are all biased by our preconceptions, individual experiences, and backgrounds. Judgments based on our intuition may guide decisions about how to live our lives, but that is no way to guide school policy.

In this chapter, I discuss the evidence as it stands, based on empirical research. There are some conclusions we can be very confident about, and others that are less certain. But overall, a great deal of research has now been conducted on school security by professionals who are trained to separate evidence from intuition. Much of it is conducted by advocacy groups aligned with particular causes—such as civil rights organizations, which are committed to reducing police presence in schools; or the National Association of School Resource Officers, which trains and advocates for police in schools. Many of their conclusions are valid, so they should not be dismissed outright, but it is important to consider their claims carefully, and balance them with more neutral research that has been more rigorously evaluated before being published. Where possible, I rely on neutral research in this chapter, using sources that have been rigorously evaluated by anonymous reviewers before publication, rather than advocacy pieces. In the end, it is crucial that this evidence has a greater role in the national discussion about how best to maintain school safety.

THE NEED FOR STRUCTURE . . .

As I mentioned in chapter 1 (and will return to again later), it is important for schools to have firm, fair, and consistently enforced rules. Students need to know what the boundaries are in terms of their behavior; they need to know that the rules will be enforced no matter who breaks them; and they need to view these rules as both written and enforced fairly. Research finds that students do not want to go to schools where the students are in charge, or where others are allowed to misbehave.[2] They want order, structure, predictability, and fairness.

This shouldn't be surprising, since it mirrors what we know about parenting. Effective parents are authoritative but not authoritarian—they are in control, they set rules and enforce them fairly, and they do so compassionately. We have probably all known children whose parents were reluctant to set or enforce rules, and who failed to learn appropriate behaviors. In both families and schools, children want and benefit from structure.

Research on school rules shows that strict rules can help prevent behavior. One recent study finds that students in schools with more strict rules on the books are less likely to be truant, more likely to graduate, and more likely to be employed years later, compared to others.[3] Yet this research does have a substantial limitation, as it looks only at principals' claims about what rules they have, not at what they actually *do*.[4] Further, these studies don't address how strict rules and punishments ought to be. If "strict" means that student misbehavior always results in some punishment, then this is likely good, since it means consistency and structure. But if it means that student misbehavior always results in severe punishment, it may not be so good. After assessing the entire field of research on this topic, a recent thorough review concluded that "severity of sanctions is not related to a reduction in problem behaviors."[5] In other words, schools with administrators who value firm and consistently enforced rules produce good outcomes, but there is no evidence that severe punishments are effective.

. . . BUT NOT STRUCTURE ALONE

The research also tells us that when it comes to school rules, structure *alone* is not good. This is the essence of a "zero tolerance" policy: a blanket rule that prescribes a harsh punishment (e.g., long-term suspension) if a student is caught violating a categorical rule (e.g., drug possession), no matter what the circumstances are. Zero tolerance rules certainly provide clear structure, but they also strip away discretion and judgment in a way that can result in silly outcomes, such as a child being suspended for bringing ibuprofen to school. Zero tolerance policies limit displays of care and compassion, and they prohibit consideration of context. In addition to resulting in silly suspensions—including the case of a Maryland seven-year-old who was suspended in 2013 when, after taking a few bites out of his Pop-Tart and realizing it looked like a gun, he pointed it at another student[6]—zero tolerance policies fail to address the reasons why students misbehave. They just punish, without fixing what is wrong. For these reasons, organizations such as the American Psychological Association have argued that we should end zero tolerance rules.[7]

Again, this should be obvious if we think about parenting. Effective parents provide structure, but when their children misbehave, they punish them with compassion and a desire to fix the problem. The fix might mean that the child needs to learn the consequences of his behavior (to himself and others), it might mean that the child has a mental or physical issue that requires medical assistance, or it could be something more mundane like the need for an adjusted bedtime.

Effective parents also choose their battles wisely. They assess each situation individually and use their discretion to decide whether punishment is truly warranted—otherwise their children might be punished so often that it loses its value and the child suffers unnecessarily. This is precisely what happens when we suspend or expel students too often, and unnecessarily, because of zero tolerance policies or simply because schools choose to punish too severely, too often.

Finally, as a result of these problems—unnecessary punishments, responding too severely to minor misbehavior, ignoring context and circumstance, and failing to address the causes of the misbehavior—overly severe punishment can also be perceived as unfair. This problem is made much worse by the fact that students of color are far more likely to be punished in school than White students, even when their behaviors are similar.[8] It is a serious problem if students perceive school rules and punishment as unfair, since the research clearly shows that school authority is considerably more effective when it is perceived as fair.[9] Firm school punishment is very important, but only in moderation; as I described in chapter 1, many schools across the United States have lost sight of moderation.

HARMS OF EXCESSIVE SCHOOL PUNISHMENT

When I talk about the harms of excessive school security and punishment, I'm often asked the same excellent question: "Since school crime began decreasing around the same time that we began suspending more kids and putting more SROs in schools, doesn't that mean it's working?" The answer is "No." Let me explain why.

The fact that two trends co-occur does not mean that one caused the other. The evidence suggests that if we had not ramped up security and punishment, declines in student crime might have been even greater, resulting in even less student crime than we see now. While the research on policing is more complex (as I discuss below), not one credible evaluation that I know of has found a positive effect of suspending or expelling more children, or of punishing rather than trying to mentor, counsel, or solve the problems that led to misbehavior. While it is compelling to believe that harsh punishments will scare children into good behavior, the evidence shows that care and compassion, and helping them deal with their troubles, works far better—here the carrots are more powerful than the sticks. Again, though firm rules are necessary, we have gone far beyond this threshold to the point where we kick kids out of school and arrest them for minor misbehavior.

Instead of preventing misbehavior, harsh school punishment has been found to cause many harms to students and schools. Perhaps the most important harm that comes from it is growing racial inequality. African American and Latino/a students are at much greater risk of school punishment than are White youths. This result has been verified repeatedly using different research methods and in studies across the United States.[10] It is undeniably true. Importantly, it does not appear that this gap is driven by differences in student misbehavior, since several evaluations are able to control for misbehavior, meaning that they factor out the role of misbehavior in their analyses by comparing students of different racial groups but similar behaviors to each other.[11]

Many educators I speak to try to deny this punishment gap, and understandably so, since they don't want to think of themselves or their colleagues as racists. And they aren't—at least not in the way we typically think of racism. Most educators I've met are fair-minded, kind people who want only to help children, and who would condemn any blatant racist action. And yet schools everywhere produce the same racially unequal result. Instead of being caused by explicit racism—school staff knowingly holding negative views about Black and Latino/a youths or intending to punish them more severely—this result is mostly due to a more subtle, implicit bias. Research shows that staff are more likely to view youths of color, particularly Black youths, as loud, disrespectful, and threatening. They may hold negative perceptions about these children's choices in music and dress, the communities they come from, or their bodily mannerisms (e.g., social distance while conversing, use of hands during speech, etc.), and these negative perceptions very subtly influence their actions.[12] (I discuss this in greater depth in chapter 3.)

As a result of this racial gap in punishment, school discipline fuels racial inequality. School punishment can harm children's future life chances, and this harm is disproportionately likely to be directed at youths of color. Paradoxically, though schools are presumed to be a great equalizer, an instrument for achieving racial equality by giving every child a free education, school punishment is one of the many causes of the uneven playing field that mars our efforts to achieve progress.

So, what are these harms that are unevenly distributed? There are several, and they have been verified consistently and repeatedly by rigorous evaluation research. Children who are suspended miss instructional time and become less likely to graduate; they are denied potentially helpful mentoring and psychological counseling in favor of punishment; while serving suspension or expulsion they have more time and opportunity for deviance; and their records and limited academic backgrounds handicap employment possibilities.[13] This process is often called the "school-to-prison pipeline." Many educators dislike this term because of the blame it puts on schools, and some researchers dislike it because it oversimplifies a complex process; though it may be problematic, this term has helped capture attention and focus it on a series of important problems.

It is important to keep in mind that suspension is most often in response to minor misbehavior, such as disrespect or defiance.[14] If schools were using suspension only to maintain safety after a violent outburst, for example, we would see it used in only a fraction of the cases that are recorded nationwide. Most suspensions are avoidable.

These findings are no longer controversial. The U.S. Senate Judiciary Committee's Subcommittee on the Constitution, Civil Rights, and Human Rights held hearings on "Ending the School-to-Prison Pipeline." The Department of Education and the Department of Justice released a "Dear Colleague" letter and several resources in January 2014 that acknowledged these problems and offered advice for preventing them. Several nonpartisan groups have recognized these problems and discussed strategies for addressing them. Some of these have included an impressive array of stakeholders, such as a recent New York City School-Justice Partnership Task Force, led by Judith S. Kaye, former chief judge of the State of New York, which included the Brooklyn district attorney, school administrators, other judges, the president of the United Federation of Teachers, and several others.[15]

PUNISHMENT, BEHAVIOR, AND SCHOOL SOCIAL CLIMATE

Above I discussed how punishment can increase inequality and result in future problems for young people, all of which are very serious harms, while there is no credible evidence that high suspension rates effectively reduce student misbehavior. The news gets even worse. A growing body of research that tries to understand school punishment suggests—but does not conclusively find—that school punishment can actually increase student misbehavior.

School social climate is the key to understanding this link between school punishment and increases in student misbehavior. *Social climate* is a term that is defined in many different ways by sociologists, education researchers, and others. But these different definitions share common ground: they refer to relationships among students, among staff, and between students and staff. Studies repeatedly find that schools with inclusive social climates have lower rates of student misbehavior than other, similar schools.[16] These are schools where students feel respected and listened to—where students believe they are treated fairly, and that they are valued members of a community. Inclusive schools actively try to strengthen bonds between students and the school or the school staff. Kids who attend schools like this are less likely than others to lash out at a community that embraces them, or to hurt others within it. If they feel respected and treated fairly by teachers and administrators, they are less likely to disrupt class or rebel against the school's authority. Fostering an inclusive climate is perhaps the most consistently verified strategy for reducing student misbehavior.

This result is probably unsurprising to anyone who understands that the best way to get respect or consideration is to give it to others. Despite being common sense, it contradicts our actions over the past three decades. One of the many demonstrated consequences of harsh school punishment is that we erode the school social climate. Harsh punishment and invasive security communicate that students are perceived as criminals and threats, not young citizens. It makes school a hostile place for many, making it *less* inclusive and alienating students from school rather than integrating them into it.

The evidence on students' responses to authoritarian school discipline is still incomplete. Though there are few quantitative studies on this, the existing research shows that students who are suspended are more likely to misbehave in the future,[17] and that schools that suspend students more frequently have higher crime rates, even while controlling for misbehavior such as classroom disorder and bullying.[18] Several studies find that students who perceive either school rules or teachers to be fair are less likely to be disruptive or commit crimes, including bringing weapons to school.[19] Though these studies consider students' perceptions of fairness more than students' actual experiences with school discipline, they illustrate the powerful and harmful consequences of students feeling alienated from the school because of unfair rules or discipline.

Qualitative research, on the other hand, powerfully illustrates students' responses to harsh punishments. Several studies, in which authors have spent years observing and speaking to young people, have shown how students can be frustrated by school rules and punishments.[20] Too often, students who earnestly want to be educated feel unwanted, rejected, or suspected of being criminals. Over time, these perceived hostilities take their toll, causing students to feel less integrated in the school, and sometimes even encouraging them to act out. While these studies are typically conducted in one or only a handful of locations, and as a result do not generalize to the entire nation, the consistency among them should leave us with some confidence in their conclusions. More research is certainly needed, but what has been conducted so far clearly shows that harsh school punishment and invasive security often result in a negative school social climate, which in turn is connected to relatively high rates of school misbehavior.

THE EFFECTIVENESS OF SROS

Up to now, I have summarized a series of conclusions that are fairly consistent and (in most cases) robust in the literature, showing that we use punishment to excess, with harms to students and schools. At this point I turn to a murkier subject, the topic with which I began the chapter: the effectiveness of police in schools (SROs). It's murkier because there is very little rigorous research that assesses the effectiveness of policing in schools, and also because there are discrepancies among the studies that have been conducted.

First, let's consider the positive consequences of stationing SROs in schools across the country. One of the primary goals of SRO programs is mentoring—putting the right officer in a school offers students a caring, responsible role model and advisor. In my research, I have always been impressed with the SROs I observed for their caring and willingness to help children in this way.[21] I have no doubt that many youths benefit from it.

Another goal of SRO programs is to better connect youths to law enforcement generally. Police departments hope that by getting to know an SRO, children will learn to see police as allies rather than adversaries. I am also convinced, on the basis of my research, that many students do learn to trust the police because of their positive interactions with SROs. As I describe in my book *Homeroom Security,* some SROs are very skilled at developing networks of student informants; these students learn to trust the SRO and to help the police respond to crime in the school or community.

SRO programs are very popular among parents, teachers, and school administrators.[22] They offer a sense of comfort and security, provide a first-responder already on campus in case of emergency, and can advise school administrators on legal matters. Whether they are popular with students is less clear. In my own research, I found that most students are happy to have an SRO, with many claiming to feel safer with one on campus. We might expect these feelings of safety to result in safer schools, particularly if it means that students would be less likely to carry a weapon to school for protection.[23] But other studies have found that students are afraid of SROs or resentful of their presence.[24] One recent study even found that students in schools with SROs are more likely to fear for their safety than others.[25]

Despite the benefits of SRO programs, it's not at all clear that SROs have a significant impact on crime prevention. Several nonpartisan reviews of the research on SROs, including one by the Congressional Research Service, point out the current lack of robust research and the need for more high-quality research on SRO effectiveness.[26] Thankfully, in 2014 the National Institute of Justice announced funding of several promising research projects that will study this issue.

Claims that SROs prevent crime are based on assumptions rather than strong empirical evidence. For example, some suggestions that SROs might prevent crime are based only on school staff members' or students' reports that they do, thus relying on personal perceptions rather than careful measurement.[27] This result is positive, in that it shows that students and staff appreciate the SROs stationed in their buildings; but it is not reliable evidence about their actual effectiveness. Individuals may be wrong about the crime that occurs, particularly when relying on their memories about how things used to be. Even if their recollection of a decline in crime is correct, this does not mean it is due to the presence of an SRO. One often-cited study, by Ida M. Johnson, argues that SROs prevent crime because she finds lower crime rates (for some crimes, but higher crime rates for others) in a sample of schools after SROs were stationed there. But she conducted this research at a time of historic juvenile crime declines across the United States generally; finding that crime declined in schools is meaningless without a comparison of annual trends among schools without SROs (which she doesn't do).[28]

In contrast, a number of recent studies using more rigorous methods suggest that SROs either have no impact on crime rates or are associated with increases in some student offenses. One of these studies finds no effect of SROs on students' reported victimization, perception of risk, or fear;[29] another study finds that schools with more SROs generally have less serious violence, but that schools with officers who carry firearms have more violence.[30] A third study, by criminologists Chongmin Na and Denise C. Gottfredson, is particularly strong, methodologically, compared with the others on this topic.[31] In this study, the authors analyze nationally representative data and find that schools that increase their numbers of SROs tend to see significant increases in numbers of weapons and drug offenses, compared to other schools.[32]

The results from qualitative studies mirror these negative findings about SROs. For example, in her study of police in a Bronx, New York, high school, Kathleen Nolan finds that police officers' aggressive tactics provoke students into misbehavior.[33] Too often, minor misbehavior, such as a frustrated student walking out of class or cursing in the hallway, becomes a criminal offense such as assault or disorderly conduct only because an SRO intervenes and escalates the problem. Victor M. Rios, moreover, finds that youths in Oakland, California, feel demeaned and labeled as criminals by a constant police presence, including in their schools, and that they often act out in ways that conform to this label.[34]

When I discuss this evidence about SRO programs' ineffectiveness in preventing crime, educators and law enforcers often respond by telling me stories about heroic actions by SROs. An SRO who takes a gun away from a child or one who relied on his rapport with a student to encourage her to talk about abuse at home are common examples. In these cases, certainly I am thankful and respectful of these SROs for their service. But it is still not clear to me that these stories are sound justification for SRO programs. In the case of the SRO who is there for a student to talk about her abuse, I wonder why other school staff members were not able to also build a rapport with that student, so that she could talk to staff other than an SRO about abuse she was suffering. This is a job for all school staff, not just SROs. An SRO who is able to do this is certainly a wonderful asset to a school, but by no means is it necessary to have armed officers in school in order to have a caring adult listener there for children. In the case of the gun at school, of course I agree that disarming a student is best left to a trained officer, not a school administrator. But these cases happen rarely— far more rarely than one would assume given the fear of school shootings (as I discussed in chapter 1). And when they do happen, the school can call the police and have an officer there within minutes. Given the rarity of such cases, and the potential problems with SRO placement in schools, the few minutes saved by having an SRO on campus does not seem a sufficient justification, on its own, for an SRO. Others may disagree with me, but as I stated above, the point of this book is to help begin a more honest, evidence-based discussion of these issues than we currently have.

Of course, another important goal of SROs is to prevent or thwart mass shootings like those at Newtown and Columbine. As I stated in chapter 1, these events are so rare that we simply don't know whether the presence of an SRO might affect their likelihood. There was no SRO stationed at Sandy Hook Elementary in Newtown, but there was one in Columbine High School—neither case is sufficient for us to generalize whether SROs are or are not effective. The few credible investigations into how to prevent these incidents focus on issues such as limiting access to firearms and better access to mental health care, and they particularly urge schools to better recognize warning signs from students who are planning a rampage attack.[35] Most students who have committed deadly rampage attacks did tell someone in advance. Some scholars therefore suggest that an SRO's presence is helpful, since a student who hears about a classmate's violent plan could tell the SRO.[36] But what is not clear to me is why the confidant is likely to be an SRO as opposed to another caring adult in the school; while more caring adults who talk openly to kids is clearly an important element of school safety, I don't see this as direct evidence that SRO programs necessarily provide that. A recent analysis of thwarted school rampage attacks finds that a positive school social climate—in which students feel comfortable opening up to adults—can encourage students to report a classmate's violent plan; but among the thwarted attacks that were studied, most were reported to another adult in the school, not an SRO.[37]

In sum, the evidence on police effectiveness is not good. I mean that in two ways. First, the body of evidence is too thin, as we need more high-quality research in order to make confident claims. But second, the results that seem to be produced by the proliferation of SROs are not what we expect or want. Without a doubt, there are benefits to having SROs on campus, which a balanced discussion should take into account—but there are also substantial drawbacks. These drawbacks rarely see the light of day, at least outside of civil rights advocacy or academic research, but they are important to consider.

SROS AND ARRESTS

One final important aspect for understanding the effects of SROs is whether their placement in schools results in more arrests at school. If it means that they are removing violent offenders from schools, making them safer for others, then an arrest is a good thing. But if it means that students are more likely than before to be arrested for minor misbehavior—the type of adolescent foolishness that used to be dealt with by a principal and dismissed—then it can be very harmful. In these cases children develop arrest records for acting like children.

Civil rights activists argue that the placement of SROs in schools expands surveillance by officers trained to spot crime and reduces the cost of an arrest, since a principal no longer needs to call 9-1-1, and that this results in more arrests, particularly for minor misbehavior.[38] On the other hand, SRO organizations such as the National Association of School Resource Officers argue that SROs are trained to respond only to crime, not minor misbehavior; thus, they only arrest students who are threats to the school.[39]

In *Homeroom Security,* I find that both arguments have merit. Most of the SROs I observed do not enforce school rules when the behavior is not illegal; they only get involved in discipline when there are grounds to suspect that a crime has been committed. And they do act with restraint most of the time, since they are there to help, not to arrest youths unnecessarily. However, their presence does indeed result in arrests for minor misbehavior that is unlikely to be reported to the police otherwise, such as disorderly conduct and minor fighting. For example, in one of the schools I studied, the principal and SRO came to an agreement that whenever two students fight, both should be arrested—regardless of context (such as who started it or whether self-defense was involved). I observed many instances where caring SROs worked hard to define misbehavior as a criminal act so they could make an arrest.

More generally, I found that the presence of an SRO influenced the school social climate in a very subtle but important way, making the school somewhat more a place of law enforcement and less a site where students' social and emotional needs are taken care of. In *Homeroom Security*, I discuss how principals delegate many issues to the SRO; some of these are clearly criminal and require law enforcement (e.g., a bomb threat posted in a bathroom), while others seem (to me) more of a cry for help. For example, I describe in detail a case where a student was taken to the hospital after drinking a large quantity of cough syrup. Rather than having this student begin seeing a counselor, the school's follow-up to the case was delegated to the SRO, whose focus was determining what crime he could charge the student with.

The research on numbers of arrests tends to agree that more SROs mean more arrests for minor misbehavior. This is particularly true for offenses like simple assault (a minor fistfight would usually be classified as this)[40] and disorderly conduct,[41] which are the most common arrest charges coming from schools.[42] One recent study, which considers school referrals to the juvenile court in five states from 1995 to 2004, finds that in four of the five states the proportion of juvenile court cases that originated in schools rose during that time.[43] While this study shows variability across states, it also illustrates that overall, arrests based at school have increased as SROs have been placed in schools across the country. Another recent analysis finds that, after taking into consideration relevant characteristics of schools (including school disorder and neighborhood crime rates), schools with SROs report significantly higher percentages of student offenses to law enforcement than schools without SROs.[44]

The problem of minor misbehavior at school resulting in arrest has become bad enough that some juvenile court judges have stepped in to address it. The most famous of these are Steven C. Teske of Clayton County, Georgia, and J. Brian Huff of Jefferson County, Alabama. These two judges describe how they saw significant increases in cases stemming from minor school infractions that entered their courts, following increased police presence in schools; yet school safety failed to improve, and graduation rates grew worse. They write:

> When police were placed on school campuses in Clayton County, Ga., in 1994, the number of referrals from the school system increased approximately 1,248%. Approximately 90% of these referrals were infractions previously addressed by administrators. Jefferson County, Ala., experienced a similar increase. During this time, school suspensions increased while graduation rates decreased to 58% by 2003. The data in both jurisdictions supported the research that increased suspensions and arrests were resulting in higher drop-out rates.[45]

Each of these judges brought stakeholders together, including the police, schools, youth service providers, and prosecutors, to discuss productive strategies for moving forward. In each county, the team agreed on a stepwise process for responding to student misdemeanor offenses. After a first infraction, a written warning was sent to the student, school, and parent; after a second infraction the student would be referred to a school conflict workshop or mediation; and after a third infraction the student might be referred to the juvenile court. They also agreed on ways to assess and treat disruptive students that avoid suspension while attempting to address the students' needs. The result was a 67.4 percent reduction in court referrals in Clayton County and a 50 percent reduction in Jefferson County, with reduced suspensions, increased graduation rates, and improvements in school safety.[46]

WE CAN DO BETTER

As I've described so far in this chapter, the existing evidence is imperfect but fairly consistent in showing that our fascination with harsh security and punishment is a bad idea. Thankfully, we know how to do better than this. There is a large body of robust and consistent research that clearly demonstrates how we can more effectively maintain school safety.

One promising strategy was discussed above: having a positive, inclusive school social climate. Helping children feel welcome, valued, and respected goes a long way toward improving school safety. Allowing them a stake in creating and even enforcing rules (e.g., with peer mediation panels), and other methods of involving them in school governance, helps students establish bonds to the school and others within it, reducing the chances that they will violate these bonds.

In addition to rethinking how students connect with schools, there are several programs in use around the country that have been shown to reduce student misbehavior. One example of a positively reviewed program is PBIS, Positive Behavior Interventions and Supports (some schools shorten it to PBS). This well-known program seeks to reward students for good behavior rather than only punish them for misbehavior; it seeks to teach students proper behavior and address the reasons for misbehavior rather than simply punish it; and it involves a stepwise system of increasing punishments rather than a zero tolerance, one-size-fits-all approach.[47]

Another promising program being implemented in schools recently is a restorative justice approach. Restorative justice is a concept that has been used in justice systems across the world and has recently gained traction within the U.S. juvenile justice system as well. The principle of restorative justice is to restore what has been lost or harmed when an offense occurs. The offender is still punished, but in a way that forces him or her to make amends to the victim, hear about how he or she has hurt the victim, and discuss why she or he committed the offense. Typically an offender will meet with the victim to hear firsthand about how the offense was perceived and what damage was done; offenders will apologize, restore the harm wherever possible, and discuss ways to move forward positively. In addition to helping victims heal, restorative justice has been found to help improve behaviors by teaching social and emotional skills.[48]

The Office of Juvenile Justice and Delinquency Prevention (OJJDP), a branch of the Office of Justice Programs, U.S. Department of Justice, has an online tool for finding school-based delinquency prevention programs with solid evidence of effectiveness. The OJJDP's "Model Programs Guide" lists programs that have been positively evaluated by rigorous research, as judged by a panel of research experts. As of this writing, twenty-four school-based programs are rated "effective" for preventing delinquency.[49] Some focus on particular age groups or populations (e.g., youths in detention center schools), and some on particular types of offenses (e.g., burglary, dating violence), while others are more general. These programs use strategies such as teaching youths better decision-making skills or anger management; empowering parents to work with schools in promoting positive behaviors; supporting students' social and emotional needs; and mentoring. They share several components, since they seek to teach youths better behaviors, equip them with the skills needed to reach these better behaviors, and offer children the family and school supports they need to overcome obstacles in their paths.

Thinking about what these programs share leads me to return to my discussion of parenting. A slight rephrasing of Hillel's golden rule, "Do unto others as you would have them do unto your children," describes successful school behavior programs. I can't imagine that many parents would want to have their children sprayed with mace for watching a fistfight in the hallway, suspended for chewing a Pop-Tart into the shape of a gun, arrested for cursing in a hallway, or punished without any effort to address why they acted up in the first place. And yet this is what we do all too often, with very negative consequences. Instead, if we treated all schoolchildren with the compassion we give our own, we would avoid overly harsh punishment, treat them with care and respect, and work with them to solve their problems rather than responding with punishment alone. We would still punish students who misbehave, but it would be in moderation, it would be coupled with efforts to fix deficits, and it would be done in a way that helps them return to school rather than encouraging them to drop out.

The research shows that these strategies can be very effective, even with some of the most difficult groups of children. A 2009 report from the New York Civil Liberties Union tells the story of six schools in impoverished parts of New York City that they call "Successful Schools."[50] These schools departed from normal policing and punishment practices of other New York City public schools and relied instead on several elements of the evidence-supported practices I describe above. Principals in these schools removed metal detectors, despite being in high-crime communities; they replaced suspension with positive behavioral responses to misbehavior; they actively involved students in school governance; they increased support for students' nonacademic needs; they worked with SROs to limit school-based arrests; they encouraged teachers to build rapport with students; and they actively sought to create climates of mutual respect and trust between students and staff. These schools showed significantly lower rates of arrest, suspension, student crime, and student (noncriminal) misbehavior, and higher rates of attendance and graduation, compared to other similarly situated New York City public schools. While these results should be verified by more rigorous evaluation, they are very encouraging, particularly since they mirror exactly what one would expect given the body of existing research.

CONCLUSION

A great deal of careful research has already looked at how we maintain safe schools. As I have described in this chapter, we do a heck of a lot *wrong*. While firm rules are certainly important, we go too far in schools across the country. We are too reliant on exclusionary punishment—suspension and expulsion—that removes students from school, where their problems only grow. Research to date has found several problems with this approach, which are now well accepted across a variety of stakeholders.

It is less clear whether the presence of SROs in schools has helped. The bulk of the evidence suggests that we have too many police officers in our schools. While they can be beneficial, particularly as mentors and first-responders in case of crisis, the evidence showing their drawbacks is growing. Certainly some schools—those few schools with documented crime problems—require SROs. But in others across the country, the drawbacks seem to outweigh the benefits.

We can do better. We can improve school social climates, improve social and emotional supports for children, and more effectively teach positive behavior to youths. We know how to hold children accountable for their behavior while helping them grow. We just need to pay attention to the evidence, so that we can move forward with as much knowledge as possible. While this evidence may not always be complete or perfect, we certainly have enough to go on; ignoring the evidence in favor of our biased predispositions is both inexcusable and harmful to children.

3 Extending Inequality

"Nobody gets to write your destiny but you. Your future is in your hands. Your life is what you make of it. And nothing—absolutely nothing—is beyond your reach. So long as you're willing to dream big. So long as you're willing to work hard. So long as you're willing to stay focused on your education."[1] This statement by President Obama to high school students in Philadelphia captures an important element of the "American Dream": that we all have unlimited potential and must work hard at school to achieve success. Of course, wealth matters too. Wealthier families can afford to live within the boundaries of higher-performing school districts or pay for private school, and they can provide additional educational experiences (e.g., travel to historic sites and visits to museums). But this quote suggests that children who are not as well off can overcome these disadvantages through hard work and focus. Universal access to high-quality education and the benefits it provides is a cornerstone of the American Dream: that anyone can lift themselves up by their bootstraps, work hard at school, and earn a bright future. After all, "Your future is in your hands."

Certainly, students who work hard at school improve their chances of graduating and securing more promising career and life opportunities. But how do we reconcile this with the now very clear reality that youths of color are more likely than White youths to be suspended, expelled, and subjected to intensive security measures at school, even when their behaviors are similar? Black children often get kicked out of school for behaviors that result in scolding when White children do them. What does this mean for the president's claim that "Your future is in your hands"? Remember, as I discussed in chapter 2, that youths who are suspended are less likely to succeed academically. This means that for Black youths, the payoff for their hard work is less certain to come, and they have lower odds of success than White youths who extend the same level of effort in school. In other words, children who act the same, focus equally on their education, and work just as hard as one another don't have the same opportunity to achieve the American Dream.

Scholars who study education and inequality have focused on issues like this for many years. We already know that our educational system is an uneven playing field, where disadvantaged youths—particularly those who come from poor families or neighborhoods, and African American youths—have more obstacles in the way of academic success than their more advantaged peers.[2] This occurs for many reasons, including (but not limited to) the facts that they have fewer resources for academic enrichment outside of school, that their schools tend to be more poorly equipped for dealing with student needs, and that school staff often misperceive or negatively interpret their behavior.

In this chapter, I argue that we also need to consider school security and discipline practices as part of this uneven playing field. The security and discipline practices that are commonly found in schools today make schools less fair, less democratic, and less just. They increase racial inequality, making it even less likely that students get to write their own destiny, or that the future is in their hands as the president stated.

In chapter 2, I briefly summarized what we know about racial disproportionality in school punishment. In the following pages I return to the topic by giving a fuller discussion of what the research shows and why we see these results. I discuss other forms of inequality in school security and discipline, and how multiple forms of disadvantage can often intersect with each other, putting some youths at even greater risk of being treated unfairly. I then contextualize this problem by connecting the inequality we see in schools to broader civic unrest in Black communities across the country, as seen in key sites like Ferguson, Missouri; Staten Island, New York; and Baltimore, Maryland.

WHAT WE KNOW ABOUT SCHOOL SECURITY, PUNISHMENT, AND INEQUALITY

Schools are supposed to be the great equalizer for American children. They are supposed to provide all children the chance to reach for the stars, as the president's speech illustrates. But scholars who study education have showed that this isn't usually how things work. Kids who start off with disadvantages when they enter school leave with disadvantages—and often these disadvantages grow worse throughout their schooling.[3]

Sociologists who study education have been discussing this problem for decades, parsing out different reasons why schools too often fail to reverse social inequality. One of these ideas that I find particularly helpful is social reproduction theory. This idea initially stems from the work of Pierre Bourdieu, who looked at how people from different groups—particularly from different socioeconomic strata—tend to have different styles and behaviors. He analyzed distinctions in tastes, such as preferences in music, dress, and leisure activities, and argued that more powerful status groups get to define which of these tastes are deemed high status. As a result, the styles and tastes that are seen more often among the wealthy are also used as markers of positive characteristics like intelligence or sophistication.[4]

Bourdieu and his colleague Jean-Claude Passeron related this theory to schools, as have several other sociologists since. The research shows how different groups of students have different styles of learning and behaving in school. Middle-class and upper-class children tend to ask more questions in class, gently challenge teachers' views and expectations, join extracurricular activities, and so on. These behaviors are *classed*—that is, they are behaviors that advantaged adults, but not disadvantaged adults, tend to teach and expect from their children. As a result, these same classed behaviors are interpreted by teachers as signs of intellect and ambition, when really they are just different (neither better nor worse) behaviors.[5] Yet the children who demonstrate these favored characteristics are perceived to be—and rewarded as—better students. In other words, disadvantaged kids are looked at as worse students, and treated worse, because of the traits that come from being disadvantaged, shortchanging their educational experiences.

I bring up social reproduction theory because it illustrates how schools not only fail to level the playing field, but also are sites where social inequality gets *worse*. When research on school punishment and security finds that our efforts to keep schools safe can increase inequality among students, it resonates with what we know about other aspects of schooling. Consider, for example, studies of school policing and punishment in low-income urban areas where most youths are Black or Latino/a. Several such studies illustrate a style of intensive policing and harsh punishment that has many negative consequences for students. Too often, youths in these schools are seen as nuisances, or even threatening, on the basis of who they are and where they live. When these youths are suspended from school for minor misbehavior and arrested for behavior such as arguing with police, they become frustrated and come to see schools as hostile places.[6] School security and punishment look different in schools like this, compared to mostly White suburban schools, with disadvantaged youths receiving less support and more hostility.[7] When we consider how suspension and arrest can hurt a child's educational career, it's clear that a different risk of arrest, suspension, and general hostility can increase inequality.

The most consistent evidence that school punishment and security can increase inequality looks at race and ethnicity. But being a member of a racial or ethnic minority group is not the only way that youths are exposed to greater risk of policing or punishment.

Race and Ethnicity

The fact that Black youths are more likely than White youths to be punished at school is no longer up for debate. Study after study has found the same result, while looking in different schools located in different parts of the country. While no single research study is immune from error, the fact that the same result is repeatedly found, even when researchers use different methods for answering this question, means we should have confidence in the answer they provide.

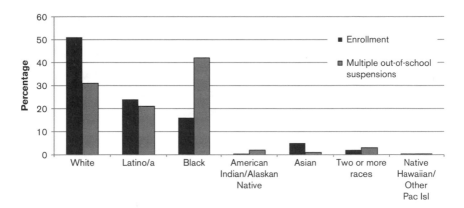

Figure 3. Student enrollment and percentage of students receiving multiple suspensions, by race and ethnicity, in school year 2011–12. Source: U.S. Department of Education, Office of Civil Rights (2014) "Civil Rights Data Collection: Data Snapshot (School Discipline)."

The research tells us that Black youths, particularly Black males, are more likely than White youths to be suspended from school. Figure 3 illustrates this for seven racial and ethnic groups, using data collected by the U.S. Department of Education's Office of Civil Rights (OCR) during the 2011–12 school year. This graph shows whether school punishment is proportionate to school enrollments, or whether students of particular racial/ethnic groups are overrepresented among youths who receive multiple suspensions. For each of these seven groups of students, I list their percentage of school enrollments nationwide and the percentage of students who are given multiple out-of-school suspensions that are from that racial/ethnic group. Here we see that White students are underrepresented among those who get punished, since they make up 51 percent of school enrollments nationwide but only 31 percent of students who receive multiple out-of-school suspensions. In contrast, Black students are overrepresented. They make up only 16 percent of school enrollments, but 42 percent of those who receive multiple out-of-school suspensions.

Of course, students who misbehave more frequently or whose misbehavior is severe are more likely to be suspended than students who behave well. If Black youths misbehave more often than White youths, this would influence suspension rates. To compensate, researchers often include measures of student misbehavior in their analyses. The risk of suspension that goes along with misbehavior rates is therefore accounted for, allowing the researchers to look specifically at the risk of suspension that corresponds to a student's racial identity, not their behavior. Importantly, several high-quality research studies that do this find that Black youths are more likely to be punished, even while statistically controlling for student misbehavior.[8]

Because of this racial gap in school punishment, the OCR has been actively engaged in studying school punishment. The OCR investigates school districts that have been found to punish youths of color more harshly and frequently than White youths for similar behaviors. They also collect data on school punishment from schools across the country, and they analyze and report on these data. A well-publicized March 2014 report from the OCR documented the overrepresentation of Black youths among suspended students, beginning in *preschool*. Though Black children make up only 18 percent of all preschoolers nationwide, 48 percent of preschoolers who receive multiple suspensions are Black.[9] While it's not clear (to me at least) why schools feel the need to repeatedly suspend a preschooler, it is entirely clear that Black children are disproportionately suspended from preschool.

In addition to individual students of color being at greater risk of punishment than White students, we also know that race matters at the school level, in shaping schoolwide practices. Schools with larger proportions of students of color tend to have different punishment and security practices. For example, in one series of studies, criminologists Allison Ann Payne and Kelly Welch find that schools with larger percentages of students of color are more likely to use harsh punishment practices such as suspension and expulsion, and less likely to use alternative practices like restorative justice, than schools with more White youths.[10] Other research finds that schools with more Black youths give out more suspensions overall[11] and are more likely than other schools to have police officers and security guards on staff.[12] One recent study finds that schools with larger populations of Black youths have higher rates of suspension and expulsion as well as higher rates of school-based arrests, compared to other schools.[13] In a study I recently conducted with Geoff Ward, we found that schools with more youths of color are more likely than others to use metal detectors, even when we statistically controlled for the reported presence of weapons on campus.[14] To date, little research has considered whether youths of color fare better or worse in different types of schools (e.g., suburban, mostly White schools vs. urban schools with mostly students of color). Nevertheless, it seems that *who* goes to a school helps shape its security practices, not just what behaviors they demonstrate.

Unfortunately, we know relatively little about whether or how these security practices are enforced differently for different students. Research on particular sites has found that Black youths and (to a lesser extent) Latino/a youths are more likely than White youths to be arrested at school, mirroring the results for suspension.[15] Yet this research has mostly been conducted by advocacy groups and reported in their self-published reports, rather than published in peer-refereed journals where it would be more closely reviewed. Further, unlike the several analyses of race and suspension, none of these research studies that look at arrest is able to statistically control for student misbehavior. As a result it seems reasonable to suspect that Black youths are more likely than White youths to be arrested at school, though we certainly need more research in order to answer this confidently.

In addition to Black youths being disproportionately punished in school, there is also evidence that Latino/a youths receive more than their share of school punishment. One recent study finds that although Latino/a students are no more likely to misbehave in school than other youths, third-generation immigrant Latino/as are at greater risk than White youths of school punishment.[16] But results for Latino/as are inconsistent across studies. Some find that Latino/a youths are punished more than White youths, but significantly less frequently than Black youths.[17] Other studies find no difference between Latino/a and White youths' suspension rates.[18]

There is considerably less evidence regarding the punishment of youths of other ethnic groups, and whether other groups are disproportionately punished after accounting for rates of misbehavior. As figure 3 shows, Asian students are underrepresented among youths punished, while American Indian and Alaskan Native youths are overrepresented.[19] Yet there has been little effort to study whether these results are related to differences in student misbehavior.

Poverty

Poverty likewise influences one's risk of being punished in school or subjected to invasive security. This occurs at both the school and student levels. At the student level, research finds that individual youths from low-income families are more likely to be suspended out of school and expelled, again while controlling for their reported rates of misbehavior.[20] At the school level, we see that schools with larger proportions of youths who receive free or reduced-price lunch are more likely to rely on security practices such as the presence of police officers and drug-sniffing police dogs[21] and to have higher rates of suspension and arrest.[22]

Sex

It is probably unsurprising that the research on school punishment tends to find higher rates of punishment for male students than for females. Male students are indeed more likely than females to misbehave, but some studies find that their rates of punishment are disproportionately high even when accounting for misbehavior. Again, the use of statistical controls allows researchers to consider risk of punishment above and beyond the risk related to differences in behavior. Similar to the results for Black youths, this research finds that males are disproportionately punished in schools overall.[23]

While girls may be less likely to be punished overall, the news is not all good for them. Female students are still punished on the basis of gender stereotypes. They are often disciplined for behaviors that may have been overlooked had they been committed by males. Girls who defy female stereotypes by being loud and aggressive, for example, can be called to task. Some suggest that schools expect and often overlook minor aggressive behavior by boys, but respond vigorously when girls engage in it, since it defies notions of acting "ladylike."[24] Again, while boys are more likely to be punished in school than girls, the evidence suggests that these punishments are not assigned only on the basis of behavior. Instead, school punishments correspond to stereotypes and implicit biases.

Sexual Orientation

Researchers have just recently begun to consider whether nonheterosexual youths are disproportionately punished in school as well. One recent study finds that youths who report same-sex attractions—particularly girls—are more likely to be expelled from school, even when statistically controlling for misbehavior.[25] Given the problems with bullying and overall hostile school climates faced by LGBTQ youths that have already been documented,[26] they seem to face a sort of double jeopardy, whereby they face bullying from peers and greater risk of punishment from adults at school. While more research on this topic is needed, results so far suggest that nonheterosexual youths may be disproportionately punished. Again, the research suggests that school punishment can be influenced by bias against nonconforming youths.

Special Education

School punishment also seems to vary based on students' status as having a learning or behavioral disability. Several studies have considered the impact of special education status on a student's risk of school punishment, and have found that students with disabilities are overrepresented.[27] A recent analysis of OCR data for 2009–10, for example, found that students with disabilities are almost twice as likely to be suspended out of school—at a rate of 13 percent, compared to a rate of 7 percent for their nondisabled peers.[28]

Intersectionality

The research I have summarized above clearly shows that for several groups of students—particularly those who are Black, poor, male, gay, and in special education classes—the risk of being punished in school or subjected to rigid security practices is greater than for others. But we also need to consider how these different statuses intersect. That is, we need to understand what happens to students who occupy multiple marginalized status positions. It's not as if a student's risk of punishment rises a certain amount for each different characteristic, in a way that we can add up.

Instead, these different characteristics intersect in complex ways, with very different experiences of people across groups. This type of analysis is known as "intersectionality" and, among sociologists, is a very influential way of studying discrimination.[29]

Few studies use an intersectional lens to understand the complex ways that student characteristics might influence school punishment and security. Yet the existing studies suggest that we need to continue in this direction. For example, scholars have found that Black males, in particular, are perceived by school staff as adult-like and threatening, which subjects them to greater punishment.[30] We also know that even though males, overall, are at greater risk of school punishment than females, the punishment gap between Black and White girls is even greater than the gap between Black and White boys.[31]

Does this mean that being female helps youths avoid school punishment—unless they are Black, and then it subjects them to greater scrutiny? Yes, it certainly does; there is strong evidence that this is the case. In a study of a poor and working-class middle school, sociologist Ed Morris finds that the intersection of race, class, and gender shapes how Black girls are treated by school staff.[32] Though many of these girls are high achievers academically, Morris finds that their efforts to participate in their classes are often ignored. Instead, teachers are more interested in scolding the girls for acting unfeminine or being too loud. He very rarely observes this sort of discipline for boys or girls of other races/ethnicities, and it usually comes when Black girls are only trying to seek attention from the teacher, such as by calling out answers or questioning the teacher. Even though these girls are punished less frequently than boys, Morris describes how they are disciplined in school in ways that reflect racial, gender, and class stereotypes. Here, race and gender intersect to put Black girls in a very precarious and powerless position.

EXPLAINING DISPARITIES IN PUNISHMENT

In sum, we know that how schools police and punish students varies across groups of students, particularly when we compare White and Black youths. But of course, a correlation does not prove causation, and on their own these results do not prove that school administrators are biased. We need to consider what might explain these disparities in school punishment.

The most obvious place to start explaining punishment rates and security practices is with student misbehavior. Whenever I discuss the problem of racial inequality in school punishment with school administrators, they tell me that they punish the students who misbehave, and that this just happens to correlate with race. Certainly there is some truth to this reasoning—it is unquestionable that youths who break school rules are more likely than others to be punished. This isn't just common sense. The research shows that reported misbehavior is a strong predictor of suspension, and also that schools with more disorder, drugs, and weapons are more likely than others to have security in place such as metal detectors, drug-sniffing police dogs, and police officers.[33]

Youths of color are more likely than White youths to suffer from negative influences, which might cause them to misbehave in school more. They are more likely to live in communities where they are exposed to violence, not to mention environmental hazards such as lead paint that might influence behavior. And as a growing body of research finds, they are at great risk of suffering from emotional trauma that can influence their behavior.[34] So it's possible that Black youths are more likely than White youths to arrive at school unprepared to learn and also more likely to act up.

But it is difficult to know for certain whether students of color, particularly Black youths, misbehave more often than White students. Most of the information we have is on suspensions, not student behavior. Suspensions are something that the school gives out, not something that students do, so counts of suspensions do not help us determine whether punishments are handed out fairly. One exception to this is the Youth Risk Behavior Survey, conducted on behalf of the Centers for Disease Control and Prevention (CDC) in high schools across the country, which asks students a couple of questions about school misbehavior.[35] Students are asked whether they have been in one or more physical fights on school property in the past twelve months, and whether they have carried a weapon onto school property at least once in the past thirty days.

In figure 4, I compare responses to these two questions of youths across each racial/ethnic group reported by the CDC for the most recent survey, in 2013. The data show no clear pattern regarding the differences between

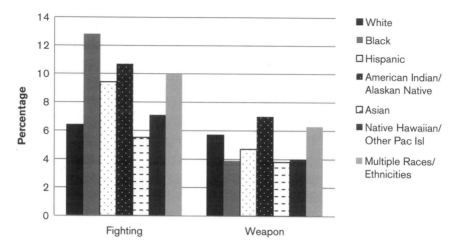

Figure 4. Percentage of high school students nationwide, by race and ethnicity, who reported fighting and weapon carrying in school, 2013. Source: Centers for Disease Control and Prevention (see www.cdc.gov/healthyyouth/data/yrbs/overview.htm).

White youths and racial/ethnic minorities. One exception to this is that Asian youths are less likely than youths of any other group to report either fighting or carrying a weapon. Black youths are the most likely to report fighting, but among the least likely to carry a weapon on school campus (3.9 percent report weapon carrying, just behind Asian youths at 3.8 percent). Hispanic youths are more likely than Whites to report fighting but less likely to report carrying a weapon.

These data are limited, but they do *not* make a compelling case that Black youths misbehave more than White youths while at school. This result echoes prior studies, which fail to find consistently higher misbehavior rates among Black students. As one study finds:

> [I]nvestigations of behavior, race, and discipline have yet to provide evidence that African American students misbehave at a significantly higher rate. Whether based on school records (McFadden et al., 1992) or student interviews (McCarthy & Hoge, 1987), studies have failed to find racial disparities in misbehavior sufficient to account for the typically wide racial differences in school punishment. If anything, African American students appear to receive more severe school punishments for less severe behavior.[36]

The data simply do not support the view that Black youths' behaviors warrant their much higher school punishment rates. But perhaps more importantly, this entire argument misses the point, for two reasons. One: as I discuss above, several carefully designed studies find that Black youths are more likely to be punished than White youths, even when the analyses account for their actual misbehavior rates. It's not at all clear that Black youths misbehave more in school than White youths—but even if they do, this does not explain the gap in school punishment between Black students and White students. Two: even if Black youths did misbehave more frequently or more severely than White youths (which does not seem to be the case), it would be counterproductive to respond with suspension, expulsion, and arrest rather than addressing the actual reasons for their misbehavior.

Several qualitative research studies help explain racial disproportionality in school punishment by shedding light on how and why Black youths are punished in schools. This research demonstrates the important role of implicit bias in shaping school punishment. School staff may not intentionally target Black youths, since few teachers espouse racist views. But Black youths are viewed differently than White youths in ways that result in more punishment. Teachers and other school staff are more likely to view the behavior of Black youths, particularly Black male youths from lower-class communities, in negative ways. These children's efforts to maintain dignity and earn respect are too often met with hostility and punishment, even when they are within the school's rules.

Several scholars have illustrated how negative responses from staff can come from misinterpretation of students' styles of dress, talk, and body language.[37] Wearing baggy pants can be interpreted as disrespectful to the school, even if the student wearing them is only trying to fit into a peer group by wearing clothes as they are worn in his community. Using one's hands while communicating—something that is more often done among Black students—can be interpreted as aggressive, even when the student has no intent to communicate this.

One recent study goes even further to consider how students' identities are punished, not just their behavior. After observing school punishment over the course of a school year and speaking to students and staff, criminologist John J. Brent finds that students—particularly Black students—

are often singled out for who they are, not just how they dress or talk. Staff learn to be suspicious of many Black students because they come from certain communities (ghettos, as viewed by staff) or they show what is perceived to be a negative attitude, and the staff target these students for punishment. While school staff are not intentionally targeting students because they are Black, the Black youths are much more likely to be perceived negatively, which lands them on the list of students who are watched closely and punished severely.[38]

Again, social reproduction theory can help us understand how this happens. When school staff develop negative views of youths because they wear baggy pants, use their hands often in talking, or come from dangerous neighborhoods, they are relying on status-based cues as indicators of a youth's character. This point is important, because it highlights how broad this process is—it is driven by social processes, not just an individual's race, ethnicity, class, sexual orientation, and so on. Unequal treatment in these cases is driven by views of what "good kids" do, what they wear, and how they behave—in contrast to what "bad kids" do, wear, and behave. As social reproduction theory tells us, these images are based on groups' social power, so that the behaviors typical of middle-class White children come to be seen as good, and the (well-intended) behaviors of lower-class Black children come to be seen as threatening.

Several independent qualitative studies—in which researchers have observed school punishment and analyzed these observations—have now come to this same conclusion about Black youths being singled out for punishment. These results mirror what we should expect given the statistical analyses I report above, showing that Black youths are disproportionately punished. Providing even more support, some analyses have considered racial disproportionality for different types of offenses. One large-scale study in particular found that Black youths are more likely than White youths to be punished specifically for "discretionary" offenses.[39] These are relatively minor offenses that do not require punishment, but for which the school disciplinarian can decide whether the particular case warrants a response from the school. On the other hand, Black students are equally likely as Whites to be punished for "mandatory violations." In other words, when school staff have more leeway for interpreting behavior, we see more racial inequality in punishment. Interestingly, this result mirrors results of research on the criminal justice system: Black defendants tend to be sentenced to harsher punishments than White defendants for discretionary offenses, more so than when convicted of other types of offenses.[40] In sum, the results from research in schools support the conclusion that school staff subjectively interpret the behavior of Black youths more negatively, and respond more vigorously, compared to how they respond to White youths.[41]

If this comes across as too critical of school staff, I apologize. That's not my intention. I firmly believe that public school teachers are underpaid, underappreciated, and overworked. I've spoken to many during my research, as well as those I know as friends, former teachers, and teachers to my children, and I have almost always been amazed at teachers' level of care, passion, and willingness to do a difficult job under duress. But when people are asked to do too much with insufficient support, they take short-cuts, such as unintentionally relying on racial bias or socially reproduced definitions of good versus bad kids.

Race and racism are everywhere in contemporary society, and they influence daily life. Implicit assumptions based on racialized stereotypes can be hidden but powerful in shaping behavior. This often surfaces through "microaggressions." These are subtle behaviors that are not intended to have racial connotations but that may, nevertheless, demonstrate the presence of racialized stereotypes, lack of respect for racial/ethnic minority group members, or assumptions about racial/ethnic minority groups' inferior status. They may include actions such as crossing the street to avoid a Black teenager, telling a subtly racist joke, or touching the hair of a Black woman to see how it feels.[42] Many well-intended Whites who might condemn explicit racism perform behaviors like this every day without realizing that they are offensive. Teachers who unintentionally misinterpret Black children as threatening, disrespectful, or hostile follow in this mold. As I discussed in chapter 1, fear of school crime and disorder has been a powerful force in the buildup of school punishment and security. Much of this fear is racialized, meaning that youths of color, and Black youths in particular, are more likely than other youths to be feared. They are at greater risk than others of being viewed as potential criminals, and often treated as such.[43]

Again, we should return to President Obama's statement that I quoted at the start of this chapter. If Black youths are targeted (intentionally or not) for school suspension, which makes them less likely to graduate and fulfill their career goals, then is the future really in their hands?

PLACING SCHOOLS IN A BROADER CONTEXT

Since the summer of 2014, the policing of Black bodies has become a high-profile, much contested issue. The deaths of Michael Brown, Eric Garner, Freddie Gray, and Sandra Bland at the hands of police or in police custody—in Ferguson, Missouri; Staten Island, New York; Baltimore, Maryland; and Waller County, Texas, respectively—touched off national discussions, debates, and protests. Being suspended from school is a far cry from being shot, and by no means do I wish to equate the two. But if we consider racially disproportionate school security and punishment in a broader context, there are clear connections between the deaths of these unarmed Black men and women and what happens in schools across the country every day.

To understand the connection, we need to look more deeply into what the protests have really been about. Watching the news media's coverage of these protests, of the "Black Lives Matter" movement in general, has been very frustrating, since too often the movement is considered to be a direct response only to the deaths of Michael Brown and others. Yes, the deaths of Brown, Garner, Gray, and Bland were the matches that lit the fires of protest, and yes, residents were irate about these incidents. But members of the Black communities in Ferguson, New York City, Baltimore, and elsewhere were speaking about much larger issues that they felt were exemplified by these police killings.

Reducing a complex problem like racialized policing down to a specific event is misleading because it distracts attention away from the broader and historical injustices facing a community. If we focus only on the details of a brief, deadly encounter, then we miss the decades of harassment and degradation faced by members of the Black community that can come from irresponsible training, supervision, and deployment of police who work in the community.[44] This bigger picture is too often missed in the effort to judge a single police officer. For example, Black residents of Ferguson were indeed angry about Brown's death, but they saw this as an example of the hypervigilant, racialized policing they had endured for years. This sentiment is expressed by NAACP President and Chief Executive Officer Cornell William Brooks, in the statement he released after a grand jury declined to indict Darren Wilson, the Ferguson police officer who shot Brown:

> The NAACP stands with citizens and communities who are deeply disappointed that the grand jury did not indict Darren Wilson for the tragic death of Michael Brown, Jr. We stand committed to continue our fight against racial profiling, police brutality and the militarization of local authorities. The death of Michael Brown and actions by the Ferguson Police Department is a distressing symptom of the untested and overaggressive policing culture that has become commonplace in communities of color all across the country. We will remain steadfast in our fight to pass the End Racial Profiling federal legislation.[45]

The protests were about years of oppression, not just a single shooting. Indeed, after Brown's death the U.S. Department of Justice (DOJ) investigated policing in Ferguson and produced a chilling report documenting racist, unjust, punitive practices unfairly directed at members of the Black community. The DOJ report is incredibly clear in documenting a history of abuse.[46] Brown's death may have been the immediate cause of the protest, but these broader historical conditions were at the heart of the protest.

The same is true in other cities marked by recent protest. Citizens of Baltimore were indeed angry about the death of Freddie Gray, but Gray's death was interpreted as part of a system of hypervigilant policing. When Black citizens who have done nothing wrong feel they have to run away when they make eye contact with police (as Freddie Gray did), there is an enormous problem. This fear of the police—which resulted in Gray's arrest and eventual death—comes from citizens not trusting that police will treat them fairly. It comes from experience with "stop and frisk" or other aggressive policing practices, in which African Americans, particularly young Black men in the poorest communities, are stopped routinely and harassed by the police because they are perceived to be threatening, disorderly, and potentially violent.[47]

School security and punishment are a part of this larger pattern. Black youths, particularly young Black men in the poorest communities, are not blind to their treatment in school. Research shows that they view their treatment in school as part of a larger system of social control, since it mirrors the way they are viewed as criminals by police and other officials. The fact that many schools now have police officers and probation officers working at them means that community policing has indeed blended somewhat with school policing. When communities subject Black youths to more policing, more surveillance, and more risk of suspension than others, they notice. They see this, and view it as part of the larger system of social control that many find oppressive.[48]

I don't mean to exaggerate the importance of school punishment and policing in this context—they are only one part of a larger system of control that is perceived as unfair and damaging by many members of the Black community. But given how widespread the problem is, particularly the problem of disproportionate suspension rates, and the fact that the vast majority of young people go to public schools, it seems reasonable to assume that it has an important effect on how young people come to see policing and punishment overall. Indeed, the perceptions of unfairness and damage are supported by the available evidence, as I describe throughout this chapter.

WE'RE ALL IN IT TOGETHER

The main point of this book is that the real problem of school safety—the over-policing and punishment of students—harms children, families, schools, and communities in ways that haven't been considered before but need to be understood. In subsequent chapters, I talk about how suspension discourages people from voting and volunteering, how unfair rules might teach bullying, how families are hurt by school punishment, and how we incur financial costs by over-policing and over-punishing students. Racial inequality in school punishment and security matters, too.

It should be abundantly clear that racial inequality in school punishment results in unfairly limited opportunities for youths of color. They are too often targeted for punishment, being kicked out of school and suffering the many long-term consequences that result, such as reduced chances of graduating and of securing stable employment. While the evidence is not as strong or as plentiful, we also see that males, LGBTQ youths, low-income youths, and special education students are disproportionately punished.

The harms of racial disproportionality extend to everyone, not just the individual youths who are affected. Above, I discussed how school punishment can fuel the resentment felt by many in the Black community toward unfair policing practices. While we can't know to what degree frustration with racially unequal school punishment specifically adds to this resentment, what happens in schools is part of the larger problem that the Black communities have been protesting. This connection is important, because we need to see the problem with school as a community-wide problem, not just as something that happens to select students.

The harms of racial disproportionality spread far beyond those frustrated with policing within the Black community. This truly is a society-wide problem about which all citizens should be concerned. On a practical level, it hurts our economy and ability to innovate when large numbers of young people are removed from school and handicapped from participating in the economy—largely based on the color of their skin. Human capital is needlessly compromised because of the over-policing and punishment of students. This siphons off talent that might otherwise be useful for potential entrepreneurship, innovations in science and technology, and other societal advances.

More importantly, racial disproportionality that begins as early as preschool highlights systemic inequality that ought to cause everyone concern, including middle-class White parents whose children are more protected from school punishment. Racially unequal school punishment and security completely contradicts the notions of equal opportunity, protections of liberty, and democratic governance on which this country is founded. Even those who aren't particularly inclined to care about the punishment of Black male youths in disadvantaged communities should be outraged at this, since it directly contradicts the American Dream of equal opportunity and success through hard work, and as a result influences the future of our nation. Is this the type of society we wish to be?

4 Hurting Families

Written with Thomas J. Mowen

It's affected me a lot of different ways. I mean, when you see your child sad and moping around. I mean, I think there were three months when he didn't even get out of his pajamas. Why? He ain't going nowhere, he ain't doing nothing. What's there even to get up to do anything for? I mean, I try to get him to go outside just to come out to the yard and get fresh air. Ain't nothing there either. It's like you try to motivate him just to go outside, and he wouldn't. It affects you. You know you see your child just going completely downhill and you can't do anything about it. But then you got all these other things you've got to do as a parent to maintain a household. You just feel stuck.

These are the words of Nora, a parent struggling with the consequences of a horrible relationship between her son, Michael, and his school. Michael, who is White and (sporadically) attends high school in a rural area outside of Mobile, Alabama, has a history of repeated long-term suspensions from his school for fairly minor misbehavior. Nora read to me the various charges against Michael as she flipped through her several-inches-high stack of paperwork from all his school punishment incidents:

Well, my son is not into fighting, or you know, the normal things to get kicked out of school for. His infractions have basically been texting in class, wearing the wrong shoes, sagging pants, stupid, stupid things.

[As she scans through the list of incidents:] One of the suspensions was for having tennis shoes on . . . one was for a third tardy, one was for a uniform violation, one was for not writing sentences in [an after school program], refusing to do classwork, refuses to complete assignments, tardy. . . .

Nora and Michael both described to me how over the past few years, Michael was kicked out of school far more than he was allowed to attend. At the time of the interview he was seventeen years old and still in the ninth grade. He and his mother told me that he had never had a problem with his schoolwork, and was actually very bright, but that he had repeatedly been unable to earn credits toward grade promotion because of the suspensions. Together, they expressed profound sadness over Michael's situation. Both mother and son realize that Michael is not going to be able to graduate from high school and are now focused on him earning a GED. But even this bears little future promise for Michael, since he is unable to do manual labor because of an injury he sustained at school, when a school bus drove over his foot (the school blamed the incident on Michael, and then accused him of faking injury). Nora laments the dim prospects Michael realistically faces, with neither an education nor the ability to do manual labor:

> Yeah he can't do construction work. He can't walk very long on [his foot]. Your feet and your hands, that is, and your head, those are your major parts, so basically. And it's all been deemed his fault. So he's going to have injuries for the rest of his life. So he couldn't even, most of the trade school is physical work, I mean they're training you to do mechanic work, things that are, uh, construction like. He can't even do those jobs now. He would not be able to do them. But he doesn't have the education to go on to college of any kind and try to get a desk job of some sort. So I mean it's basically changed his entire life. And I mean I try to be positive, and [turning to Michael] I don't even know what positive direction to push you in. I mean he was doing Tae Kwon Do and all that, and he couldn't do that anymore after the foot injury, cause he couldn't use his foot to kick and stuff. So he couldn't go to the tournaments and stuff like that. So even the interest that he was in, he couldn't, he couldn't have that outlet anymore either. [Laughs] . . . Now this is all we do, we just wait for the babies [Michael's younger siblings] to get home. That's it. Ain't it fun?

Michael's suspensions have taken a major toll on him. He told me that he no longer trusts teachers or school administrators, since he feels that they have all been cruel and unfair to him. He has lost contact with his social networks, since he is at home all day rather than with them or sharing their experiences, and when he does attend school he is among much younger classmates, whom he has trouble relating to. And as one might expect, he is very depressed and hopeless about the future. Though his story is a bit more extreme than most others, the effects of his school suspensions are predictable, given what we know of school punishment and the consequences for students—such as school failure, employment problems, and so on—that were discussed in chapter 2.

But the existing literature on this problem doesn't address Nora's suffering. During our interview Nora was close to tears several times as she described the pain of watching what has happened to her son, trying in vain to advocate for him, and observing how Michael's situation has affected their entire family. In this chapter, I turn to Nora rather than Michael and highlight the effects of school punishment as they are experienced by families.

It's difficult to say why Michael has had such a difficult time. During our meeting he was thoughtful, respectful, and kind. Based on our meeting, it's hard for me to imagine him being violent or even disruptive in class. And his offenses at school were all nonviolent (other than one incident in which he claims to have been playfully rough-housing with his stepbrother), according to Nora. Michael claimed that he just doesn't fit into a "redneck" school, since he doesn't wear what he called "redneck" clothes, such as hats with fishing hooks and "redneck boots," and he is punished for being different. Regardless of why he has been banished from his school for such long periods of time, it was difficult to witness his pain and the suffering of his mother.

LISTENING TO PARENTS

In November 2012 and January 2013, I visited Mobile to talk to parents of children who had been suspended or expelled from school. I did this research with Thomas Mowen, a professor at the University of Wyoming, who is my coauthor on this chapter. We were invited to visit with and speak to parents who had been working with the Southern Poverty Law

Center on a project to teach parents their legal rights regarding school punishment and how they can best advocate for their children. We met with seventeen families. Most of our interview respondents were mothers, though we also spoke to grandmothers and occasionally a father, grandfather, aunt, or uncle; in some cases the student would join in the interview. Most of our respondents were African American, and the majority were either unemployed or worked at blue-collar or service-sector jobs, suggesting that they were a fairly marginalized group, overall, in terms of socioeconomic status.

During these interviews, we asked about their experiences when their children (or grandchildren) were punished at school. Our goal was to learn more about how school punishment and other school safety efforts can affect family life. As we describe below, we heard about the frustration, stress, and anxiety that parents undergo when their children are suspended or expelled. We heard about how families suffer when parents must miss work to pick their children up from school, and when the troubles with the school lead to conflict among family members. We learned about how parents—like Nora—can give up on their efforts to work with the school, and how they can even give up hope for their children's future, as a result of school punishment.

In the appendix, I discuss how we contacted parents and our methods for completing these interviews. One aspect of our research that is important to mention here is that we recognize that the parents we spoke to do not represent all parents across the United States. We interviewed motivated parents who had chosen to participate with the Southern Poverty Law Center—and who then consented to be interviewed by us. For the most part they felt aggrieved by schools and wanted to talk about the pain they had experienced. Certainly, we would have heard very different stories—much less dramatic, with positive views as well—had we interviewed a random selection of public school parents. But our goal is not to describe the average family, or to understand how common it is that families suffer as a result of school punishment. Instead we wish to know what it is like for families that have been affected. These interviews give us a glimpse of the harms to families that can be caused by school safety practices gone wrong, which is an important element to the story, especially since the consequences of school punishment are typically ignored. When one considers the fact that growing numbers of studies document the use of excessive and unfair school punishment practices, this element of the story seems even more important.

PRACTICAL MATTERS

School punishment can affect families—particularly parents—in many very practical ways. One family with whom we spoke was actually separated as a result of seventeen-year-old Tyler's troubles. Tyler's mother, Alyssa, told us that he was being bullied by a group of students and even had his car stolen, at his high school, which made him afraid to go to school. The school district granted Tyler a transfer to another school, but the principal at the new school was hostile to the transfer and revoked it after three weeks under the pretense of punishment for tardiness and truancy. Alyssa explained how Tyler was removed from the new school on false pretenses:

> ALYSSA: [The principal at the new school] revoke his transfer because he said that Tyler was skipping school, being late . . .
>
> INTERVIEWER: Was he?
>
> ALYSSA: No. Because he . . . he called me one day. No, I texted him, and he said—and [I] said "[Tyler], I just call the school and they said you are not on roll." I said "you're not on roll, you're grounded." And then he texted me back saying "Mama I am at school." And he took a picture and show me that he was still in the class. So that's why I'm saying they trying to provoke him, so they can revoke his transfer.

After the new school revoked his transfer, his old school refused to accept Tyler back. Tyler wanted to go to school but was left with no options for public school, and Alyssa was unable to afford private school. Alyssa then tried to send him away to live with family members in order to continue his education:

> He wanted to go to school. He tells me every day he wants to go back to school. And I tried to, to send him to Atlanta with his aunt to see if she could find a program for him so maybe go back in school. . . . But I don't know

what with that. Last night I was on the phone with my uncle and his wife in Birmingham and she told me that she was going to get on the phone today and try and see what she could do. She call me but I couldn't answer it, I was at the dentist with my son. But sometime I'm going to call her back when I can and see what she say. But I'm willing to take him up there for them to stay with her so he can go to school because I really don't want him to be in this environment.

Of the seventeen families that participated in our research, there were three that experienced separation, a child no longer living with his or her parents because of school punishment. Practically all other parents with whom we spoke also feel the bite of punitive school treatment, but in other ways. In particular, having a child suspended from school for either the short or the long term can severely interrupt a parent's ability to care for other children, maintain employment, and manage a household.

This is clear if we return to Nora and to how the strain of Michael's suspensions affects her life. Nora is married and has five children: Michael, two other teenage boys, and two smaller children ages three and five. Both of the younger children are disabled, one with a severe physical disability and the other with a severe developmental disability. Nora's marriage is her second; she became a widow five years ago and remarried. One of her older sons is currently in the hospital recovering from a motorcycle accident. As she tells me, "In the past five years, they've all played tag for who goes to hospital. Everyone has been in the hospital at least once. [To Michael:] You've been in there twice. [One of Michael's brothers has] been in there, [another brother's] been in, [Michael's sister]'s been there, [Michael's other brother]'s been in there. So in five years, we're on a first name basis with the hospital people. It's sad."

Nora's life is very difficult. Michael's school experiences make it considerably more difficult. Each time he is suspended, she needs to pick him up from school or risk his being sent to a juvenile detention center.

INTERVIEWER: What happens when the suspensions are going on? Take me through what happens, do they call you?

NORA: Yeah they always call me to come get him. And if I don't get there within a certain amount of time they send him to Strickland.

INTERVIEWER: What's that?

NORA: Youth center.

MICHAEL: Juvy.

NORA: So basically if I don't come get him by their time schedule, by when they want him out of there, then they're gonna put him in jail and I have to get him from there. I mean, you know, I mean they even let other kids ride the school bus home if they don't have a ride to get home. Some people work in this country. If you can't come get your kid you have to pick him up from jail, how stupid is that?

As a result of this threat, Nora went so far as to keep Michael home some days:

I mean I actually did keep him home some days because, you know, "I can't come get you if you get suspended. I gotta be at the hospital. I can't come get you. And they're gonna lock you up, they're gonna put you in juvenile if I'm not there to come get you. So let's just not go to school today in case something happens." Who keeps their kid out of school for that reason? It's come to that point that it is so ridiculous. It's not like my kid is even having emotional problems where he's fighting every day. He's getting suspended for stupid stuff. But I don't want him to spend the weekend in jail just because I couldn't pick him up at school. Because I had other things to do. You know, it's not like I wasn't concerned with him. It's just I have other things, medically. . . . It's kind of like you have to choose the importance of your child. Who's higher up on the totem pole to worry about today? A kid's medical needs override stupid suspensions. So let's just not go today. I mean, I've never really heard any other parent have that excuse not to send their kid to school. I mean it's, it was at that point. I mean I would actually, I would sit there by the phone all day long, at that time I had four children in school, my special ed one too, because my little one hadn't went yet, and basically you would answer the phone and like "Which one? Which one are you calling about today?"

As she described here, Michael's trouble in school requires time on her part—both to pick him up at school when he is sent home, and to supervise him once he is suspended—that competes with her other family obligations.

Sometimes Michael's school punishments directly interfere with Nora's strategies for managing her difficult circumstances. For example, Nora is often in the hospital with her youngest child, and on those days she depends on Michael to pick up her five-year-old from the school bus stop. When he does go to school, Michael keeps a phone with him, so that his mother can call if she needs his help. But if the school finds the phone, they confiscate it for a week. Or consider Nora's account of her efforts to manage her father's affairs after his death:

> My father passed away recently. And the first day [Michael] went to school, he got suspended that day for texting in class. That day he went back to school after like three or four days of being out when my father passed. And I was going and taking care of family business. So I was all the way across town when they called to come get him, and I was finally back close enough to school and they said "Well if you're not here in five minutes, then you'll have to go pick him up in juvenile hall that he'll be arrested." Like I'm not doing enough today.

Other parents, as well, described how the time that is consumed by their children's school punishments can make difficult family circumstances even tougher. Several discussed the impact of repeated school punishment on their ability to hold down jobs. These parents don't just have to visit the school every now and then, they go there *often*. School exclusion requires multiple meetings rather than a simple school pickup: the parent may need to meet with the principal or school board, and they may be required to accompany their child on his or her return to school. These meetings are time consuming, often located far from their homes or workplaces (at the school district building, not at their local school), impossible to plan in advance, and often require immediate responses. They complicate work schedules tremendously.

One parent, Teresa, works off the books cleaning houses, but has had to turn down many jobs: "Well, it affected me financially because I wasn't able to carry on my daily activities. Which, what I mean is that I wasn't able, you know, I had to be here with him, and worry about him being here, and what's he gonna do."

Veronica, who is a nurse, has accommodated demands from the school by taking on the night shift at the hospital instead of working days:

VERONICA: And I was coming up there [going to the school because of school punishment] fairly, too much. I mean, it was coming to where I switched jobs, you know, I had to take a night job.

INTERVIEWER: Because you were going to the school so much?

VERONICA: Yes. At least three times.

INTERVIEWER: You shifted jobs because of the school discipline?

VERONICA: Absolutely. Absolutely. Absolutely. And I'm still working nights now. You know, they're not in the household with me during school hours, but I'm still at nighttime. Can't do it. Couldn't do it. Because once they know that you are involved, oh they gonna, they blow your phone up twenty-four hours. Every little thing. Every little thing. He's doing this, he's doing that, he's not doing this, he's not doing that.

Later in our interview, Veronica expanded on the subject of missed work:

> You know that the suspensions affect the family in so many different ways. From the elementary school to high school, it affects the parents. Because the parents have to rearrange their schedule, they are taking off for suspension. I mean, that's another thing you have to take off, for the school board, when they decide you have an appointment. So you already took off for the child, when you have to come pick them up, then you have to take off because the child is suspended, then you have to take off again to appeal it, you know, in between phone calls during the day. How do you maintain? You still have to feed your family! You know, work so that you can maintain, and it's a constant interruption.

Relatedly, parents may be concerned about what their children do all day when suspended, and feel the need to watch over their children, ask that a family member or friend watch their children, or pay for a babysitter. Even if their children may be old enough that they do not need constant supervision, parents may be concerned about trouble their children can get into if left alone all day. Another interviewee, Kiara, described how she tried, but wasn't always able, to watch her son, who is now expelled from school and facing arrest on sexual assault charges:

INTERVIEWER: So all those times that he was suspended, what happened when he came home? What did he do?

KIARA: Well, sometimes I would have to leave him, like, you know, after he turned eleven, I would have to leave him at home. Or with the babysitter or something because I was trying to work. And go to school myself. So, you know, he really had nothing to do. Well, he fell to the streets.

Driving to and from school meetings also places a practical demand on parents. Nora described how she was frustrated that the amount of time it took to try and meet with school officials resulted in wasted time and fuel money: "A few times, I went there [to the school] all day . . . come back the next day just to wait for them to hurry up . . . but no, now I have to come back here [to the school] tomorrow, waste gas when we could've done it the day before."

Most of the parents with whom we spoke are fairly poor, which means that they are more likely than middle-class parents to work at low-wage jobs, and less likely to have flexible schedules or job security. The practical demands of frequent school visits, school board meetings, and supervising their suspended children have important impacts on their schedules, work lives, and incomes. In this way, already disadvantaged families are significantly hurt by school punishment.

EMOTIONAL AND PHYSICAL HARMS

Even more than the practical difficulties discussed above, the most common problem caused by their children's school punishment that parents reported to us was emotional pain, such as stress, fear, and a sense of guilt. Some parents also told us that the emotional toll caused symptoms such as post-traumatic stress disorder and hair loss. Again, we return to Nora, who expressed her frustration, sense of failure as a parent, and pain at having to watch her child endure what they both view as needless suffering:

> I mean, I wanted better for my kids. You know, but I mean, if you don't have a good start, you're not gonna have a good end. And now we're just now starting GED school, and he's almost eighteen years old, and it's work in your own pace. So he may end up being there for another two years, two or three years. You never know. So he didn't get his four years of education. I mean, it's sad.

Evelyn, whose seventh-grade daughter was repeatedly suspended, described the stress she feels because of her struggles to work with a school system she perceives as hostile:

It's traumatizing . . . It's . . . You know when they were on the *Today Show* . . . they were talking about the soldiers and post-traumatic stress. When you go through it from year to year just dealing with the [school] system . . . it's almost like you feel almost like a post-traumatic stress type of thing. I have been so stressed out. . . . The hair. I cut my hair off because my hair would just come out. Your nerves, you know. Even though I went to the police department and the lawyer wrote a letter on my behalf. When I went back into school, I just, you couldn't see it but I was just a nervous wreck. I never thought in a hundred years I'd have to endure this just to have her educated.

She also described her frustration in the following terms: "They strip you, they try to strip you of your pride, of your dignity and your integrity to where you're so beat down you have no more fight in you. As far as pushing your child through, your rights, you don't have any. You know. They, it's very seldom, that you meet just a nice principal who's there."

Other parents also reported physical effects. Alyssa said, "[It's] hurt me too because we're all scratched out. I be up all night, I can't sleep [I've] lost weight, my hair's coming out of the side. But it's hurtful, it's, it's hurtful, it's really hurtful." Some parents feel physically sick when dealing with school administrators. As Nora stated, "My stomach would turn when I would see caller ID. You know like when you see caller ID, the dread. My stomach would turn when I would see the caller ID. Like I don't have enough already, like, what now?"

Teresa also vented about her frustrations as a parent whose child is suffering as a result of school punishment. Here she described how the principal only sees the bad in her child, and how the harsh treatment leaves her feeling that she has no rights as a parent:

[Her son] felt like the principal never seen the good in him, that he seen the bad in him. And that he didn't really have a chance to, you know to really, say "Look I'm a good kid." Because the principal wouldn't allow him to say you're a good kid. And you know, well that, that was definitely the attitude that I got from the principal, that, you know, "I only seen the bad in all the kids." You know, "I'm looking at the bad things about him. And I never seen the good in them." Say, "Look man, you, you, you got, you're smart. You know, you've got something to give this world." Now, they don't say that in schools anymore, that's not their attitude. And that's the way it affected him. You know, he went back to school, and he, oh my God the principal rode him. The principal, rode him, rode him. You know what I mean, he was on his case all the time.

He was going and you know, going through his backpack, just like that. Went to his backpack. Took his cell phone from him several times. Um, um, and them um, kept it. I had to go to the school. He said "Mama he just got it out of my pocket. He just walk up to me take it out of my pocket. Said 'You're not supposed to have that at school.' And, um, 'Over where I can see you.'" And just all the time. All the time. So toward the end of the school, I asked him, I said "Are you ever gonna see the good in my child? Are you ever gonna try to look into that good and manifest all that good and bring that out, and shine that out with me?" "Well, when I see some." [Laughs] Right front of him, he said that right in front of my son. But you know, you gotta be careful how you talk to these principals, because they got the power. I mean, they honestly have the power over you, really they do. I mean, what it all boils down to it, and they know they do. Because I mean, and that's what so upsetting as a parent because you feel like you don't have any rights even though they're your children you're sending them there, hoping they're being taken care of.

Other parents with whom we spoke mirrored this frustration but also spoke about how it causes them to feel as if they are bad parents. Kiara described how her son and his siblings were each punished repeatedly for very minor infractions, and how his treatment made her feel:

> KIARA: I just don't understand. And it's never been where my children have attacked a teacher or anything. These are little petty things that they have been suspended for. My son has been suspended for maybe a uniform violation, or something like that. The wrong color socks. You know, just something real, real petty.
>
> INTERVIEWER: Why do you think they do that?
>
> KIARA: [Laughs] I, I, I don't know. I just feel like they don't have the patience for the kids or—I can't begin to understand what's going on. . . . It makes a parent look bad when they do these things. It makes it seem like you're not doing your job as a parent. So. . . .

A moment later in the interview Kiara returned to this theme and stated: "You gotta, you gotta do what you need to do for your kids. It just, it makes you feel real bad, like you're not a good parent or you're not doing a good job at raising your child. You know, it's hurtful to your image."

Parents also told us that school discipline often complicated their relationships with their children because they saw their children as the source of their aggravation, even if at some level they recognized it was not the child's fault. Teresa highlighted this when she outlined the partial blame she places on her child:

> It [school discipline] can cause friction between the mother and the child . . . the parent and the child. Because now the parent is upset with the child all the time because the child is that nail. You know it's like a thorn in my side. You know every time I'm getting this phone call for you, and now all the time the child is a problem. It's the relationship the child has with the school, or the school's relationship with the child, is causing friction in the household. Now the child's confidence is low, because he is the black sheep of the family, and it's causing a little family thing going on. You know, so that's breaking up the family dynamic as well. You know, so now you're looking at, you are labeled as a bad child. When you're just slipping in math. You know? So now you're bad. And that trickles down. So you have the self-esteem issues.

Roberta, another parent, echoed this: "It's embarrassing to have to go to school, you're [her son is] 14 and I'm tired of having to get over [to the school] . . . and talk to these people about you not sitting down and being quiet. . . . I'm basically at my wits' end and about to take him out of school." Moments later, she returned to this theme: "You know these people [school officials] are watching your every single move, just go to school and be quiet so I don't want to keep going to the bat for him if he's not doing what he is supposed to do."

These themes were expressed repeatedly across interviews. The parents we spoke to feel beat up: that they were doing their best to work with the school, but the school had turned it into a fight, and the parents were overmatched. They feel that their efforts to advocate for their children were met with disdain, leaving them stressed, frustrated, and hurt. As quoted above, Evelyn went so far as to equate how she feels after doing battle with the school to post-traumatic stress disorder. As a consequence of these emotional and physical tolls, parents often feel a rift in the relationship with their child.

GIVING UP

The effect on parents of this stress and frustration is an important consequence of school punishment. Many parents expressed to us that as a result of their frustrations, they have given up. They may have given up on advocating for their children in school, given up trying to participate in their children's education, or given up on schooling for their children altogether. Kiara, for example, described her response to the punishment her children received: "Oh, as a parent it is very stressful. It makes you not even want to deal with them. I've been in a stage where I didn't want to deal with them." Other parents echoed this same sentiment, saying that they no longer want to deal with the school.

One response to this sentiment is to ignore the school, or refuse the school's calls. As another mother, Alecia, stated in response to how she feels about her daughter, Tanya, being punished repeatedly:

> Sometimes, a lot of the times I just won't answer the phone. If I see the school calling I know what they're calling for: to come get Tanya. And one time they call to come get Tanya, right after we went to court, and she was like "Ms. Harold said to come get Tanya." And I said "Tell her I'm not comin' to get Tanya cause I just left court, let her stay all day." I get in trouble behind her doing this and doing that and ain't nobody trying to get no help for her. And I, I don't really have no time to up and do this every day of the week. And I don't know. I can't even say. So, I'll just be glad when she graduates. She gonna be done.

Other parents expressed a loss of trust in the school as a result of their experiences. In this interview, Carol, the mother, and Deinya, the aunt, described their response to how Carol's son was treated in school, particularly in response to multiple suspensions for dress code violations (not having his shirt tucked in):

DEINYA: And we're supposed to have a relationship with the teachers as parents. You shouldn't be angry at the teachers. We're supposed to have a relationship because, of course, these teachers spend more time with the children during the day than we do because we're working. And we shouldn't be angry at them because, you know, there are some parents out there that don't care.

CAROL: We should be able to trust them!

INTERVIEWER: And you don't feel like you can?

CAROL: No!

DEINYA: Oh, no.

CAROL: No. I have become so, um, defensive, you know, and I had to
school him in the mornings. I had to say, well, "Don't forget to
do this, don't forget . . . you got your belt . . . tuck your shirt in—
no that's not tucked in right."

While our interviews were focused primarily on parents, these parents
occasionally talked about how their children had given up hope, too.
This is clear in Michael's statements at the start of the chapter, in which
he freely expressed his lack of hope either in receiving an education
or establishing any form of sustainable career. Others, too, expressed similar sentiments, such as Roberta discussing the experiences of her son
Mark:

I think this is Mark's last year in school. He has just given up hope. He's just
like, "Just find me a job then I'll work." And I'm like, "You're just 14." So . . .
And I even asked him if you want to go to another school and he said all of
his friends are there. And I'm like "Your friends will be leaving you next year,
but I hate to say but I don't think you gonna make it past the eighth grade
. . . not at [his current school]."

Most of our respondents talked about their children's experiences with
school punishment, and the school's hostility toward them, as an indignity
that they had to endure. Parents expressed anger and frustration that
their children were targeted for minor infractions like dress code violations, or even for nonexistent misbehavior, and because school staff seem
unwilling to listen to them and hostile when they were able to speak up.
They feel that they and their children are unwanted by the school, and
that the school views them with contempt. While many parents and children choose to endure their frustrations and continue to interact with
their schools, others do not.

It's important to realize how harmful it is to degrade parents in a way
that alienates them from the school. Having parents who participate in
their children's school experiences—whether volunteering, advocating for
their children, helping with homework, raising funds for the school, or in
other roles—is essential to student success. Research finds that when parents are more involved in their children's education, children tend to have
higher grades, better attendance, fewer suspensions, higher levels of self-
esteem, and less drug use, alcohol use, and violent behavior.[1]

These consistent research results mirror what I am often told by teachers and school administrators when discussing school safety. School staff often ask me for suggestions on how to better involve parents in the school, or they might complain about a lack of parental involvement, which makes their jobs more difficult. Either way, the school staff members with whom I interact clearly see families as a crucial element for student performance and school safety. And yet, as illustrated in this chapter, school punishment has the potential to discourage parental input, thereby removing one of the most important resources for schools. The parents with whom we spoke learned over time that they are not wanted in the school, and nor are their children.

CONCLUSION

As I argue throughout this book, the real school safety problem is that we have gone too far with some school punishment and security practices, resulting in a host of negative consequences that have previously been overlooked. In this chapter we have seen how school suspension and expulsion can affect parents and entire families. As these interviews show us, school punishment can be very damaging, with harms that go well beyond the students themselves. Already marginalized parents—those who work for hourly wages, single parents, or those who face other barriers due to poverty and racial exclusion—are even further marginalized by some school disciplinary practices.

Keeping in mind that low-income children and youths of color are more likely to be punished severely in schools, it is clear that the harms suffered by families fall disproportionately on those who are already disadvantaged socially and economically. The parents we spoke with reported practical issues such as having to find child care, adjusting their work schedule, or worrying about transportation to and from the discipline hearings. Many of these parents highlighted emotional and physical effects such as increases in stress and anger, and even loss of hair and sleep. As a result, many reported giving up. They had given up on trying to intervene on behalf of their child and, in some cases, on education for their child entirely.

When parents are involved in the educational process as partners with schools, good outcomes should happen. Because of the importance of parental involvement in schools, it is important that we better understand parents' involvement in and responses to school punishment—and yet prior analyses of school punishment have failed to consider how it affects parents. As I discuss in other chapters, excessive school punishment and security practices have negative implications for students, but this chapter demonstrates that the same disciplinary mechanisms also hurt parents and entire families.

Schools and families must work together. Parents need to trust schools to take care of their children and educate them; in turn, schools must rely on parents to prepare students to learn, and to support the school's efforts. Excessive punishment, and hostility from the school toward students and parents, limits parents' ability to cooperate with the school. This makes it more difficult for schools to teach and for parents to care for children.

5 How Schools Teach Bullying

Written with Katie A. Farina

Bullying has become more of a concern in recent years among the news media, school administrators, parents, and policy-makers. This is important, since bullying can be very harmful to children. But the discussions and policies that result from this concern have neglected to consider how school authorities bully students under the guise of school security and punishment. In this chapter we describe how unfair rules and punishments might actually teach bullying behaviors and put children at greater risk of bullying victimization.

To begin, consider what I learned in my discussion with Alecia Underwood, a mother of nine children and one of the kind people whom I interviewed in Mobile, Alabama. During our interview she talked about the difficulty her children have had in their public schools. She described how in the third grade her daughter Tanya was repeatedly locked up in a dark, windowless closet while at school. Tanya's offense was trying to leave school—she was never violent to other students or staff. Alecia told me that Tanya kicked the wall of the closet repeatedly and, over weeks of being locked up, eventually kicked a hole in the wall that let her exit. As Tanya herself reported (with her mother present):

INTERVIEWER: What were you doing to get put in there?

TANYA: I get mad and try to run away from school. . . . They get somebody to haul me and put me in the room.

INTERVIEWER: Then they'd leave you in the room? How long did they leave you in the room for?

TANYA: The whole day.

INTERVIEWER: The entire day?

TANYA: Yes.

INTERVIEWER: Did they let you use the bathroom?

TANYA: No.

INTERVIEWER: Did they let you eat lunch?

TANYA: They slide it under the door.

INTERVIEWER: They slid it under the door, and they'd leave you in the room for the whole day?

TANYA: Uh huh [yes].

INTERVIEWER: That's gotta be kind of scary.

TANYA: With the lights off.

INTERVIEWER: With the lights off? No windows?

TANYA: They cover them up.

INTERVIEWER: How many times do you think that happened?

TANYA: They put black papers on the windows to block my looking through.

INTERVIEWER: Do you think that happened maybe ten times or more?

TANYA: More.

INTERVIEWER: Twenty?

[Here Alecia noted that Tanya was in the room so many times that she was able, over the course of *weeks*, to kick a hole in the wall.]

Alecia also talked about how one of her older children was singled out for punishment by an assistant principal while in middle school. This son, Marcus, was a quarterback on the football team and had never been in trouble in school. But one day he was given a five-day out-of-school suspension for talking in class. Alecia told me:

So I called back to the school that afternoon and I talked to the head principal. And I said "I don't think it's fair that he get a suspension for five days when he's never been in trouble, never been in a fight, never done nothing but play sports and do what he's got to do." So she kind of overruled the assistant principal and told me that she'd send him back the next day and they ain't gonna put it as a suspension.

Alecia then described how this angered the assistant principal who was overruled by the principal, and he took out his anger on Marcus. He told Marcus, "I'm gonna get you Underwood. You gonna' get it," and he watched closely over Marcus and punished him for minor infractions. One that Alecia mentioned was that the assistant principal did not let Marcus play in a football game because his shirt was not tucked in while he was at school earlier that day; the assistant principal threatened to suspend Marcus if he showed up for that night's game.

This is what bullying looks like, and I have no doubt that similar acts would be described as bullying if they happened between two students. Definitions of bullying vary considerably, but they tend to include a few common criteria: bullying involves the use of coercive power over some-one who is less powerful than the aggressor, it is repeated over time, and it is intentional.[1] The actions of school staff against her children described by Alecia (and by Tanya) certainly meet these criteria. In both cases school staff acted aggressively against a child who held little or no power, the behavior was repeated over time, and it was clearly intended to communi-cate that these children are "trouble," or unwanted.

Tanya's experience of being incarcerated in a dark closet is pretty extreme, and both of the above examples involve only one family. While all of the families with whom I spoke in Mobile described aggression and mistreatment at the hands of school staff, few incidents matched the severity of this repeated cruelty toward a third-grader. Yet many of them also described incidents, repeated over time, in which school staff were intentionally cruel to their children. For example, Roberta told us that her son, Mark, reported the following:

He said this teacher constantly calls his name and says "Don't be like Mark, don't do this like Mark." And he recorded it because the teachers is picking on him and there's nothing I can do about [it]. . . . One teacher even said he went on a field trip and his pants were sagging and he had on a wife beater shirt on and I'm like, "That's not even true!" I buy Mark's clothes. He cannot sag his pants because I buy his clothing. And all of his pants fit around his waist. And she's like, "Maybe he just pulled them down" and I'm like, "That cannot be true!" We don't even own wife beaters in my house. My husband doesn't even wear wife beaters, so unless he walked out the door and put it on, there is no way he wears it. She says maybe he took it from somebody else and I'm like, "Really, lady?" I think she was just making something up so she would have to agree with the rest of the teachers at the parent–teacher conference.

Another parent, Carol, described an incident that happened when her son, Darius, was seven years old. A boy gave him a broken flash drive, which Darius then played with. Darius's teacher saw him playing with it and was angry to see that it was broken, since it was hers. The teacher did not care that Darius didn't take it, didn't know where it came from, and thought it was a toy. She paraded the two small boys from classroom to classroom and forced them to publicly admit that they stole property. As Carol described:

> And he had to tell each class that he was a thief. And when [the teacher] walked him to the car he looked like he wanted to say something. And I said "You better say right now whatever it is, don't wait till you get home and start explaining. Tell me right now." And he said where the [other] little boy was [and how the other boy just] gave it to [Darius] and I said [to the teacher]: "Do you know this?" And she said "Yes. [The other boy] did admit to giving it to him but possession is nine-tenths of the law." I said "He is seven years old". . . . This is what she said to me—she marched him from classroom to classroom and made these two little boys tell each class that they were thieves.

Later in our interview, Darius's aunt, Deinya, described how Darius responded to a more recent incident, when he was expelled from school for having a cell phone with him: "And that night he cried because he can't understand why the teachers are so against him when he knows that he hasn't done anything wrong." Clearly Darius felt bullied, which had an emotional effect on him; as we describe below, bullying can indeed be very harmful to students.

These are not isolated incidents among the stories we heard. Several parents told us that teachers and school administrators explained their children's frequent punishments simply by saying that their kids are "bad."

We repeatedly heard stories about children punished at school for minor infractions because teachers or administrators didn't like them and had the power to kick them out of school, and that it was done in an intentionally demeaning manner. One parent, Veronica, explained how she saw it as an intentional strategy to make overcrowded classrooms more manageable:

VERONICA: I had a substitute teacher tell me one time that when they're having an overflow, that's the tactic. They get them out. They know who they can provoke, they provoke the bad ones, get them out so they can have a good day. You know.

INTERVIEWER: Trying to thin out the class?

VERONICA: Yeah. So you know it's an issue.

These experiences are not limited only to the families I met in Mobile. When doing research for my book *Homeroom Security,* I was struck by how commonly school staff members bullied students. Teachers and administrators are human, and it's predictable that they would lash out at students who cause them the most trouble, who make their lives difficult. Unfortunately, though, this often looks a lot like bullying: adults (who have significant power over children they oversee) repeatedly demean certain students as they express their frustration. Consider the following interaction, which I reported in *Homeroom Security* (see p. 130), between a student, Mark, and a school disciplinarian, Mr. Brook:

A tall, thin, Black male student came in the office and sat down next to a female student who had been waiting to see Mr. Brook. Mr. Brook (a White dean of discipline) continued to work on his computer during the following conversation:
  Mr. Brook: Why are you here, Mark?
  Mark: I want to file a complaint.
  Mr. Brook: Against who?
  Mark: Against a teacher—she told me to shut up. [The female student laughed.]
  Mr. Brook turned to look at Mark and said, "Mark, I'm gonna' put it to you like this—shut up!"
  Mark: Naw, man, if I had said that to her, I would have been in trouble, so she shouldn't be able to say it to me.

> Mr. Brook: Mark, it's funny that you mention that. [Mr. Brook dug
> through a pile of paperwork.] Because I have a referral for you here that says
> you told a teacher to leave you the f- alone.
> Mark: Naw man, I didn't say that. I just told her to go do her job some-
> where else.
> Mr. Brook didn't respond to this; he turned his back to Mark and kept
> working on his computer.

This interaction is fairly typical for disciplinary interactions in many schools and resembles descriptions offered by a growing number of in-depth studies.[2] It's not abusive, like Tanya's solitary confinement during the school day, nor does Mr. Brook deliberately target Mark, in the way that the assistant principal targeted Marcus for retribution. But I would argue that this still looks a lot like bullying. Mr. Brook uses his power as an adult school employee to tell Mark that Mark doesn't matter. He does it with his words ("Mark, I'm gonna' put it to you like this—shut up!") and with his body language (turning around and ignoring Mark). I observed interactions just like this with some regularity, often with the same youths being repeatedly demeaned over time by the same staff members. This kind of bullying involves adults yelling at children, imposing their will on children, and demeaning these youths because they can—because they have more power.

Throughout my research, as I have observed and heard reports of students being bullied by adults in school, I have become concerned about what effect this may have on students. In this chapter, which is coauthored with Katie Farina, a professor at Cabrini College, we discuss an important and previously overlooked consequence of current school safety practices: increased rates of bullying victimization.

A BROADER VIEW OF BULLYING

Bullying is both common and harmful. Estimates vary, but research tends to find that between 15 and 30 percent of youths are either bullies, victims of bullying, or both.[3] Being a victim of bullying is associated with increased risk of substance use, violent behavior, unsafe sexual behavior, and sui-cidal behavior.[4] While it's not clear whether being a bully to others causes further problems, or whether both bullying and other problems are results of deeper-seated issues, bullies are at risk of a host of future problems, including delinquency, substance abuse, school failure, depression, and eventual criminal conviction.[5]

The definition of bullying has expanded in recent years to include cyberbullying, acts such as posting negative information about someone on social media or other electronic forums. Actions by school staff like the ones we described above are perhaps even more similar to a traditional definition of bullying than many cyberbullying acts are, but because we tend to think of bullying in school as something that happens only between children, such actions by adults usually aren't seen as bullying. They should be. Bullying by school staff may not include the giving of wedgies or swirlies, taking of lunch money, or physical violence—but the expression of hostility and power through actions and words is bullying nevertheless.

Traditional views of bullying are also limited because we often tend to see it as something rooted in individual deficits. We tend to see bullying as the result of a particular youth who has some problem, such as insecurity or cruelty, that makes him or her lash out at others. In their book *Beyond Bad Girls*, criminologists Meda Chesney-Lind and Katherine Irwin argue that most bullying is a result of *group*-based power, such as racism, sexism, homophobia, or social-class antagonism, yet educators and others tend to see bullying only as the result of choices made by individual students to dominate and humiliate others.[6] Dr. Farina and I agree with the broader perspective, that bullying can be caused by group-level antagonisms, and we are interested in how bullying is shaped by how entire student bodies are treated. In this chapter we build on Chesney-Lind and Irwin's argument to show that bullying rates can also be increased when schools have unfair rules and punishments.

Certainly, our society has come a long way in recent years toward recognizing the extent and harmfulness of bullying among youths. Since 1999, nearly every state has created new laws to prevent bullying and/or punish bullies.[7] Much of the more recent attention on bullying is the result of tragic cases of suicide, like that of Tyler Clementi, an eighteen-year-old Rutgers student who killed himself in 2010 after his roommate posted a video of him kissing another man. The federal government has taken steps such as launching the "It Gets Better Campaign," designed to empower

LGBTQ youths who may be victims of bullies, and the stopbullying.gov website. An important part of this trend is the implementation of bullying prevention programs. The most popular of these is the Olweus Bullying Prevention Program, founded by Dan Olweus, whose program has been shown in several studies to help prevent bullying.[8]

This is all good news. It means that adults are no longer willing to dismiss bullying as a normal part of growing up, they recognize the harms that can come from bullying, and they have implemented evidence-based programs in response. But traditional views of bullying are still limited, as they focus only on students, not on adults as well, and most often on individual students rather than groups. Granted, the Olweus Bullying Prevention Program does consider entire school climates, not just individual students, as part of what needs to be addressed in order to prevent bullying. But in this model, "school climate" refers to whether other students are accepting of bullying as opposed to disapproving of it, and whether they are willing to intervene to stop a bullying incident. We need to understand that bullying can result from *adults'* actions within schools as well.

Recall from chapter 2 that an inclusive school social climate is important for preventing student misbehavior, and that invasive security and overly harsh punishments are harmful to the school social climate. In this chapter we argue that bullying needs to be included when we think of these harms of negative school social climate, since a school's efforts to prevent crime can actually encourage bullying if schools' rules and punishments are unfair or too harsh.

BULLYING TEACHES BULLYING

It is probably no surprise that being bullied teaches children how to be bullies themselves. Many bullies are also bullying victims.[9] It makes sense that children often copy the behaviors they observe or mistreatment they receive: victims of childhood abuse are at increased risk of being abusers themselves,[10] just as children whose parents smoke (or drink, or vote, or so many other behaviors) are more likely than others to smoke (or drink, vote, etc.).[11] Reasons why are complex and varied. Some would explain it by arguing that children learn to imitate those around them, particularly those they admire; others would state that children learn specific coping strategies from their parents or other adults around them (e.g., drinking or violence in response to stress); others might argue that observing negative behaviors makes them less daunting, reducing the disincentive to engage in them; and so on. The point is that children learn from their environment and from how they are treated by authority figures.

Shouldn't we expect this to happen in schools, too? Granted, school staff are less immediate role models than most parents and have much less influence on children than their parents do. But given how much time young people spend in school, it makes sense that the behavior of adults in school might influence students' behavior. If students went to schools where adults openly smoked cigarettes, wouldn't we anticipate higher rates of youth smoking than in smoke-free schools, for example?

We see no reason why bullying would be any different. If children attend schools where adults bully them or their peers, it makes sense to assume that these schools have higher rates of bullying than others. If individual students are subjected to excessively harsh punishments or hostile school climates in the name of tight security, one might expect them to be at increased risk of involvement in bullying.

SCHOOL RULES AND BULLYING

To answer the question of whether school safety efforts might actually increase bullying, we analyzed data from the 2009 School Crime Supplement (SCS) of the National Crime Victimization Survey (NCVS).[12] The NCVS is one of the largest, most consistent, and most commonly used sources of data on crime in the United States and is conducted by the U.S. Department of Justice (Bureau of Justice Statistics). Each year, almost 160,000 randomly selected individuals from across the country, in 90,000 households, participate in the survey. Survey respondents are interviewed twice a year about any crimes that have been committed against them, to gain a picture of criminal victimization. The SCS is conducted every two years as a supplement to the NCVS, to learn about school-related victimizations and student perceptions of crime and safety from household members ages twelve to eighteen. These individuals must be in primary or secondary schools and have attended school at least six months prior to the interview.

This dataset is well suited for our purposes, but it's not perfect. It is strong in that it's a large, nationally representative survey that asks about bullying victimization and school characteristics. This allows us an in-depth view of how school safety climate is related to bullying. But there are two important weaknesses as well. One is that we are able to measure bullying victimization, but not bullying behavior itself; we can determine whether someone was bullied, but not whether they themselves bullied others. Though these measures are imperfect, they still let us consider how school policies and practices shape the levels of bullying that occur in schools overall. The second weakness is that it's difficult to measure adult bullying of students in a survey. We began this chapter with the story of Alecia Underwood's two children to illustrate what bullying looks like—but these are the kinds of stories that are best captured through interviews or observations, not surveys.

Although imperfect, the available measures are good enough to use in examining how school safety practices are related to bullying. Specifically, we use five questions that all students are asked in the survey, measuring each student's agreement that, in his or her school, (1) everyone knows what the school rules are, (2) the rules are fair, (3) the punishment for breaking rules is the same no matter who you are, (4) the rules are strictly enforced, and (5) if a rule is broken students know what punishment will follow. We also include a scale that measures whether teachers' responses to student behavior are lenient, balanced, or firm; this is based on students' responses to two questions that ask about how frequently students disrupt class and how frequently teachers punish students. Finally, we look at schools' use of a variety of security practices, such as police officers or security guards, metal detectors, locked entrances or exits, locker checks, ID badge requirements, and surveillance cameras.

Again, the details of our research methods are described in the appendix and are not needed here. But it is important to note that we ran statistical models to predict students' risk of either physical bullying, verbal bullying, or cyberbullying. Our models include many control variables, such as demographics (sex, age, race, etc.), school characteristics (whether gangs are present, drug/alcohol availability, etc.), and student characteris-

tics (history of fighting, grade point average, etc.). Including these variables means that we statistically remove their influence to better analyze
how school safety practices are independently related to the likelihood of
being a bully's victim.

The results confirm our fears. Students who agree that the rules in their
school are fair are less likely to report any in-person bullying, verbal bullying,
and cyberbullying. Further, students who report that school punishments
are predictable (they agree that "if a rule is broken students know what punishment will follow") are also less likely to be victims of any type of bullying.
These results are clear, and exactly what one should expect given the volume
of research discussed in chapter 2. They tell us that schools where rules are
fair and fairly enforced tend to be safer for students, with lower risk of bullying victimization. In contrast, when children go to schools where rules are
unfair and unfairly enforced—like the schools attended by Tanya and Marcus
Underwood—they are at greater risk of being victims of bullying.

Figure 5 illustrates these results. It shows the estimated probability
(from 0 = no chance to 1 = certain) that an individual youth reports any of
the types of bullying victimization we measured, based on their agreement
that the rules in their school are fair. We measured bullying in four ways:
any in-person bullying, any in-person physical bullying, any in-person verbal bullying, and any cyberbullying. For each type of bullying, each bar is
lower than the one to its left, meaning that as students voice more agreement that their school's rules are fair, they are less likely to be bullied. For
example, the estimated probability of any in-person bullying for a student
who strongly disagrees that school rules are fair is .37; but for a student
who strongly agrees that the rules are fair, this probability goes down to .21.

Figure 5 also shows that the probability of any student reporting cyberbullying is low, and that it gets even lower when students view the school
rules as fair. Though this is outside the point of this chapter, the low overall rate of cyberbullying suggests that recent concerns about rampant
cyberbullying are well intended but may be overstated.

Our results for teacher punishments are also interesting. We find that
when students report that teachers are too lenient (i.e., students frequently
disrupt class but teachers infrequently punish them), they are at greater
risk of being bullied. As I've mentioned several times in preceding chapters, it is important that students who misbehave receive punishment, so

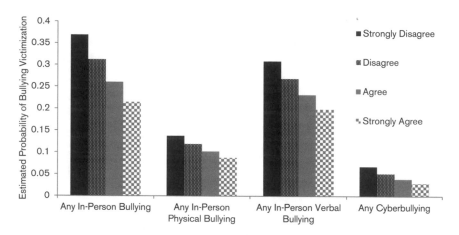

Figure 5. Estimated probability of bullying victimization, by level of agreement that "the rules are fair."

long as it is fair and addresses students' reasons for misbehaving. Ignoring student disruption does no good, and our results show that bullying is higher in schools where this happens.

This highlights a crucial point that tends to be overlooked in discussions about school safety. When it comes to setting rules, punishing students, and maintaining security, the issue shouldn't be seen as all-or-nothing. Locking up third-graders like Tanya for trying to leave the school is abusive and harmful—but so is ignoring students' misbehavior. Children need to learn from their mistakes by being taught proper behavior and being treated like valued members of a school community who have made mistakes. Pointing out that excessive school punishment hurts students, families, and communities does not mean that we shouldn't punish misbehaving students. Instead, it means we need to do so fairly and intelligently. This is precisely what our analyses of bullying victimization show.

CONCLUSION

Chapter 4 demonstrated how excessive punishment of students hurts entire families. This chapter has extended that argument, showing that excessive punishment has another important harm that hasn't been considered before: it can increase the risk of bullying victimization. After illustrating how school punishment can resemble bullying, we find that the risk of being bullied is greater in schools where rules are unfair or inconsistently enforced.

As our results indicate, and as many other researchers have documented, one of the problems of the excessive school security and punishment used across the United States today is that they are seen as unfair and are unevenly enforced. Not only are the rules excessive (and hence unfair), they are also used to single out youths of color and others perceived as "bad kids," making unclear what punishment will follow when students get into trouble. As my coauthor and I demonstrate through the use of multivariate statistical analyses, these important corollaries of excessive school security and punishment show an important relationship with the likelihood of being bullied. A very recent study using the same data series, but measuring both bullying and school discipline slightly differently, comes to the same conclusion. Julie Gerlinger and James C. Wo find that students who believe that the rules in their school are fair and strict, punishments are consistent, and teachers are respectful to students, are less likely to be victims of physical bullying, relational bullying, or verbal bullying.[13] The consistency of these results, despite different measurement and analytical approaches, leaves us more confident that the results are valid.

We have argued that excessive school security and punishment resembles bullying and can teach students how to bully. Our statistical analyses extend what we learned from parents' descriptions of how their children were mistreated in school, finding that students in schools with unfair and unevenly enforced rules are at greater risk than others of bullying victimization. This does not in any way mean that all or even most school staff members are bullies. On the contrary, during my research I have observed many wonderful, caring adults who put in extra hours and go far out of their way to help children, without bullying. Mr. Brook (described in a less-than-flattering way at the start of this chapter) often acted with care and compassion as well. It is a shame if some negative behaviors by some school staff come to characterize students' perceptions or the results of external investigations like this one. At the same time, there is sufficient evidence at this point to show that bullying-like behaviors by school staff are common and harmful. My intent is not to tarnish the reputation of schools or blame overwhelmed and under-resourced staff. Instead, I wish to spur a productive discussion about improving school safety in ways that help students without also hurting them and their families.

6 Civic Participation in the Future

Written with Thomas J. Catlaw

When describing her interactions with her daughter's school in Mobile, Evelyn had the following to say about the school's hostility to parents' participation in and criticism about the school:

> They try to put you in a box, to put you in your place. It's pretty much an attitude . . . it's a certain way, a demeaning way that you are supposed to get it. And then sometimes they are just outright bitter and nasty and you're supposed to be quiet because they don't like it if you are a talkative person. . . . If you want [your child] to stay in the school the next year, you are supposed to sign some paperwork requesting to remain at the school if you're a transfer student. Now if they don't like you, they can scratch you off. But the paper does not require that [the school] give any type of detailed information why. . . . If the child had excessive absentees, or excessive disciplinary problems, those types of things. Or if the parent did not want to cooperate. Nothing is in detail as to what exactly they're talking about so I've confronted central office about this particular form and he said, well they don't have to give any details they just don't want you over there, they don't have to. Well this is being used as a retaliation against parents. They don't give you anything to answer you . . . so . . . so. . . .

She describes a situation where commentary is frowned upon and dissent is punished. In this chapter, Thomas Catlaw, a professor at Arizona State

University, and I consider this kind of treatment at the hands of schools, and ask what lessons students learn from school discipline and security that guide their future behavior. We find that school punishment has effects years down the road, as it can discourage formerly punished students from participating in civic and political life as adults. This adds another piece to my overall argument that excessive school punishment and security can have negative consequences that are deeper, broader, and longer-lasting than prior research has acknowledged.

SOCIALIZATION

Schools are future oriented. Their entire purpose—other than providing child care—is to prepare children for the future. As a society, we so strongly believe in this future orientation that we force all children to go to school (or home school) until at least age sixteen. But what, specifically, do schools teach children? The most obvious is the academic curriculum: reading, writing, math, social studies, and natural sciences. At a minimum, most children learn basic skills they will need to function as adults, such as reading comprehension, basic math, and knowledge of important historical events. For some children, those who are fortunate enough to continue to higher education, their K–12 academics prepare them for college courses by teaching them necessary preliminary material.

Yet this academic content is a small portion of what children learn in schools. They also learn skills, behaviors, and attitudes that they take with them throughout their lives. One of these is the ability to perform critical thinking. A hallmark of a strong educational background is that students learn to ask good questions about the world around them, and to dig deeper into what they are told rather than accepting at face value everything they hear, see, or read. Critical-thinking skills are necessary for innovation, since they lead entrepreneurs in any field to reject the status quo and create, just as they propel scientists to question conventional thinking and conduct original research. Another important skill that children can learn in school is good study habits. Not only are good study habits important for academic success, they also translate into skills needed for the workplace: time management, organization, and an ability to set priorities.

In this chapter, I focus on a similar type of learning: socialization, or the process of learning how to act. Socialization is a central part of the school experience. One type of socialization, perhaps the first type that young children learn, is how to get along with other children. Parents of preschoolers and kindergartners, for example, may be very concerned that their children learn to share toys, make friends, and express themselves clearly. Parents of older children may focus instead on their children's ability to get along with others and stand up for themselves in the face of conflict.

Even if parents don't actively think about socialization as an important part of schooling, it still factors into many of our thoughts. As an example, consider the aversion many people have to homeschooling. Even though it may be growing in popularity, particularly with online resources available to help educate youths at home, still only about 3 percent of American children are homeschooled.[1] For many, homeschooling appears odd, or deviant, because it means that kids are secluded and don't learn how to interact with other youths.[2] My point isn't to debate the merits or drawbacks of homeschooling, but to point out that most parents see the importance of peer socialization, even if they don't call it by that name.

Our concern with socialization is also a central reason why we place such importance on athletics. Certainly, sports help children stay physically fit and instill physically healthy habits in our children, which is of growing importance in an era of obesity concerns. But the value of athletics goes beyond physical fitness. While participating in sports, children also learn skills like teamwork, healthy competitiveness, perseverance, leadership, and the ability to cope with both success and disappointment, all of which help prepare them for their future roles as adults. As Paul Caccamo, director of Up2Us, a coalition of community sports programs, states: "Sports are more than a game; they are a set of life lessons. Kids growing up without them are really disadvantaged. . . . Kids who participate in sports attend school more, are more community and civic minded, get in less trouble, and tend to be more successful in the workplace."[3] Clearly, it is widely recognized that our job as parents and educators extends far beyond teaching academic subjects.

LEARNING TO BE CITIZENS

My children attend the public elementary school for which our house is zoned. One of the main lessons they learn there is to remember the "three R's": respectfulness, readiness (to learn), and responsibility. Teachers discuss the three R's at the beginning of the school year and repeatedly throughout the year, posters hanging in the classrooms remind students of them, and every month the school has an assembly where the students from each class who best demonstrate each of the three R's are each given an award. Of course, it will be easier for teachers to teach and students to learn if everyone is ready for lessons, acts responsibly, and is respectful of others. But the three R's are about much more than facilitating academics; they represent an effort to teach children appropriate behavioral standards. The socialization process isn't just about learning skills, or how to get along with other children—it is also about learning rules and appropriate behavior as defined by adults.

Research on education shows that socialization into expected behavioral standards (much like teaching the three R's at my children's school) has been a central mission of public schools since at least the late nineteenth century. In his widely read book *The One Best System*, David Tyack describes the creation of the modern school and the goals of the educational reforms that directed its development. Beginning in the 1890s, reformers began dismantling what they saw as erratic and haphazard schools (think of a rural, one-room schoolhouse, which taught whatever it wanted, however it wanted) and replacing them with modern, bureaucratic school systems. Their intent was to help society, especially rural society, adapt to life in the new era of industrialization. These reformers saw schools as the perfect tool for socializing children—and their families—into the rules of a rapidly changing society. This was seen as particularly important because of the enormous numbers of immigrants coming to the United States around that time, who, reformers thought, needed to learn the rules of American society in order to get along in it. Reformers saw schools as the answer because schools could teach children the skills and habits they needed, such as punctuality and following directions, to be factory workers and productive citizens.[4]

Others, too, have argued that in addition to teaching reading, writing, and arithmetic, schools have always socialized children into future roles as citizens. Scholars have shown that schools did this by preparing some children to become "blue-collar" workers and others to be managers or "white-collar" workers.[5] This finding may be less accurate today, as the world of labor is no longer as neatly divided between blue-collar and white-collar workers.[6] But those who study schools agree that schools seek to teach children behaviors and habits that prepare them for their future roles as citizens in American society.

Our history of racially segregated schools and gendered educational practices also illustrates the powerful influence of schools as a force of socialization. Racially segregated schools were essential to maintaining broader racial segregation, since they helped establish firm barriers between Black and White youths that would carry over into adult life. Certainly, part of the reason for the strong resistance to legally mandated school desegregation during the civil rights era was the understanding that school desegregation would help dismantle other racial boundaries. Girls as well have traditionally been educated in ways that conform to gendered expectations that limited their career paths to teaching, nursing, and other typically feminine paths. While girls are now encouraged to enter STEM (science, technology, engineering, and mathematics) fields and other fields traditionally occupied by men, there is still considerable evidence that they are treated differently than boys in school in ways that socialize them into traditionally feminine gender roles.[7]

One very important behavior that school socialization can shape is whether young people grow into adults who are engaged with their communities. Whether or not people vote, volunteer, and participate in community activities is in part shaped by their experiences in school.[8] Motivated by the concern, voiced most famously by Robert Putnam in his book *Bowling Alone*,[9] that adults today are connecting with each other less, scholars have begun to think about how schools can shape civic and political activity. If we want to produce citizens who actively participate in democratic society, we must teach them democratic practices.[10]

What do democratic practices look like in schools? They embrace core values of democracy: that all citizens are entitled to a voice, that problems are solved collaboratively, and that all citizens are valued. Some school administrators and teachers are fantastic at treating students with these values in mind. In such schools and classrooms, children's views and voices are respected and students are involved in making decisions about the school. This doesn't mean that the children run the school, as adults still have the authority and responsibility to direct and instruct students when their opinions or desires may not be healthy or productive. But it does mean that students participate actively in how the school is run, that they are listened to, and that they are respected. These are core features of a positive school social climate, which we know is one of the best ways to promote school safety (see chapter 2). Following these democratic practices also socializes students into democratic participation—it teaches them how to use their voices productively to contribute to society.[11]

Now consider the quote from Evelyn at the start of this chapter, in which she discusses the hostility toward parents' voices that she feels from the school. This environment is clearly not one that encourages democratic participation. What lessons do students who attend this and similar schools learn?

SCHOOL PUNISHMENT AND CITIZENSHIP

Schools are perhaps the most important way that children become socialized into their future roles as citizens. It's where they learn the rules for participating in society, and how to interact with others. What, then, do they learn from contemporary school punishment and security? As described earlier in this book, rules and punishment have become a central component of schools. Excessive punishment, which has become more common in schools across the United States, hurts families and might even teach students harmful behaviors like bullying. Students who are punished in school are at risk of several negative outcomes, such as dropping out, arrest, incarceration, and unemployment.[12] But no research has looked at what citizenship lessons they learn from this, or how school rules and punishments socialize them into future adult roles. This is an important omission when we know that (1) schools have such an important role in teaching us about our adult roles and (2) school rules and punishments are a central element of how schools work and what they teach children.

As described in earlier chapters and in my book *Homeroom Security*, in practice school security and punishment can be very *un*democratic. As I observed repeatedly while doing research for that book, school disciplinarians all too often fail to listen to students or take into account their needs and perspectives. Instead they apply rigid rules without regard for individual situations. It rarely matters *why* a student acts up, so long as there is evidence that he did what he is accused of. A teacher acting inappropriately (e.g., by publicly embarrassing an academically struggling student) doesn't matter; only the student's response to it does. For example, I observed many cases in which a student's punishment would be decided on before the disciplinarian even met with the student—clearly, the student's voice and needs were not considered.[13]

Describing the rigid policing evident in New York City public schools, Aaron Sussman makes a similar argument. He states:

> The second way school police deny students the opportunity for civic participation is through the suppression of traits and values that allow one to thrive within a community and advance in public society. This suppression takes multiple forms. First, through excessive, disproportionately enforced discipline, school police cause nonwhite students to mistrust law enforcement, lose faith in the legal system, and hold negative views toward public institutions. As Justice Stevens stated, "The schoolroom is the first opportunity most citizens have to experience the power of government. . . . The values they learn there, they take with them in life." Second, . . . underfunded nonwhite schools tend to penalize traits that are valued in civil society, such as creativity, assertiveness, and independence. School police compound that suppression by making it risky for a student to do anything to stand out, including being outspoken and engaging in free expression. Lastly, the traits that these schools and the police reward—subordinacy and conformity—are not traits primarily favored for community leaders or politicians.[14]

Here he is primarily focused on policing practices in schools that serve mostly students of color, as these students are most likely to bear the brunt of school punishment and security.

In one sense, schools borrow a page from the criminal justice system, which often mandates the formal limitation of citizens' democratic rights as a part of their punishment. As of 2014, forty-eight states prevent individuals incarcerated for felony offenses from voting; thirty-five states maintain this ban on voting after individuals are released, while they are on parole; and thirty-one states do not allow felons on probation to vote.

Other states maintain the ban on voting well after these citizens have been released from prison, probation, and parole.[15] School punishment is not equivalent to incarceration, and discouragement from civic participation is not equivalent to losing the right to vote. But the comparison shows a precedent for punishment to entail a loss of democratic rights and privileges.

Rigid, undemocratic school punishment practices are evident in the interviews with parents quoted in chapter 4. For the parents we spoke to, the undemocratic nature of school punishment affected entire families, not just students. Their stories describe their experiences with hostile school administrators who refuse to listen to them and who make decisions without any input from student or parent. As Evelyn strongly expresses at the start of this chapter, these entire families are not allowed to participate in the school discipline process. Behavior like this by a school teaches a powerful lesson: that the school is not interested in democratic participation.

Other studies have found similar stories of undemocratic treatment at school. One example is in a report from the Center for Information and Research on Civic Learning and Engagement at Tufts University, titled "'That's Not Democracy': How Out-of-School Youth Engage in Civic Life." One student is quoted in the report as stating:

> We are built, you know, to believe, you know, we have these rights, we have this, we have that. But when it comes down to, it's like, it's able to be flexed, you know. Like, you have these rights, but not on this property. Or, you can do that, but not over here, you gotta go that way. That's unfair. . . . If we're standin' as a collective group protesting something or trying to better ourselves, you know, I believe it should be encouraged, instead of being discouraged . . . that discourages us from doin' the right thing, and then we start thinkin', ah, well when we get the right thing we get the wrong answer, so when we do the wrong thing are we gon' get the right answers?[16]

Lessons like this are very important for how youths learn to be citizens. As discussed above, school is where young people learn how to be citizens. They experiment with different identities (and haircuts, styles of dress, etc.) in an effort to discover who they are and how they wish to get along with others. This is all part of the socialization process, whereby they gradually adopt the behaviors they will carry with them into adulthood. If we want to mold young people into adults who vote, volunteer, and participate in their communities, then we should be teaching these habits and rewarding these behaviors during adolescence. When schools offer children the opportunity to experiment with democratic participation, and schools reward their efforts by listening and encouraging their participation, students learn to repeat these behaviors. On the other hand, if youths are discouraged from having any say in how they are treated, if a democratic dialogue is discouraged in their schools, then we will likely see them become apathetic, disengaged adults. Schools have a powerful socializing effect, and this can be used to promote future adult democratic involvement or to discourage it.

VOTING AND VOLUNTEERING YEARS LATER

Based on what we know about school socialization, and what we know about the undemocratic nature of school discipline, it makes sense to expect that students who are treated undemocratically are less likely than others to be active citizens years later. These youths learn that they are *problems,* not potential *solutions*—they are treated as nuisances who get in the way of orderly, effective schools. If their experiences teach them that they have no voice, and that they must accept authority without argument, then why would they come to learn that they have any opportunity to change the world through civic or political action?

With this in mind, Thomas Catlaw and I wanted to look at how school punishment shapes future behaviors. Our concern is that undemocratic school punishment teaches youths a model of citizenship that is, well, undemocratic: that one should keep to oneself, accept authority without complaint, and forget about trying to change things in the world around them.

No previous research has considered whether students' experiences with school punishment shape future democratic practices years later. But we can look to a closely related topic, law enforcement, as a guide for what we might expect to see. Researchers who study policing and youth have found that when children believe they have been treated unfairly by police, they are at risk of developing "legal cynicism." This means that their experiences with police influence how they view laws, and particularly whether they view laws and police as legitimate. Youths who have negative experiences and as a result see laws or police as illegitimate are less likely to ask police for help or to follow laws.[17] In other words, youths' experiences with laws and law enforcement socialize them into future behavioral patterns.

To consider whether experiences with school punishment shape future democratic behavior, we used data from the National Longitudinal Survey of Adolescent to Adult Health, which is commonly known as "Add Health."[18] The Add Health survey is huge and has been used by many researchers to conduct very important studies. It began in 1994–95, when 20,745 children in grades 7–12 from across the country were randomly selected to participate in it. Researchers interviewed these children, their parents, and administrators at the schools they attended. Researchers then followed up with these youths three additional times, for a total of four "waves" of data collection, the most recent in 2008–09.

This dataset is well suited for addressing our concerns, for several reasons. First, the fact that these youths are followed up over time, well into adulthood, means we can see how their experiences as children are related to their behaviors years later. Second, it is a large, nationally representative survey, which means that we can be very confident that the youths selected for the survey look a lot like youths across the country in 1994–95 generally. Third, the questions youths answered during the first interview include whether they were suspended in schools, and questions from later interviews include whether they vote and volunteer in their communities.

We conducted statistical analyses to look at whether individuals who are suspended in school are less likely to vote or volunteer years later, when they are well into their twenties. Importantly, we statistically controlled for dozens of variables that might shape both whether a child is suspended (including their use of drugs and alcohol, whether they have committed any of a wide range of crimes, their grades, whether they participate in extracurricular activities, etc.) and whether they vote or volunteer as adults (including whether their parents vote or volunteer, their socioeconomic status, how connected they are to their communities, etc.). This let us look at how suspension is related to voting and volunteering years later, after removing the influence of all these factors. In the appen-

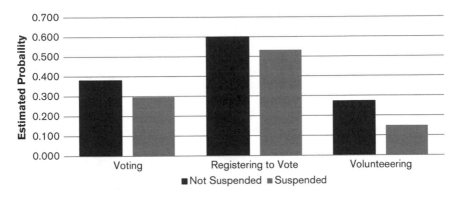

Figure 6. Estimated probability of voting, registering to vote, and volunteering.

dix, we discuss our research methods in more detail for those who are interested.

The results of our analyses are clear: children who are suspended in school become adults who are less likely to vote, register to vote, and volunteer in their communities. Figure 6 shows the predicted probability (ranging from 0 = no chance to 1 = certain), based on these analyses, that youths who were suspended and youths who were not suspended vote, register to vote, and volunteer, as measured in the third wave of data, when they are eighteen to twenty-six years old. For example, the predicted probability of having volunteered for someone who was suspended as a student is .27, but it is only .15 for someone who was suspended, all other factors being equal.

We continued by looking at whether these results hold for the final wave of data, which were collected in 2008–09, when the survey respondents were twenty-five to thirty-three years old. They do: we again find that youths who are suspended are less likely to vote and volunteer frequently.

Having found that suspension predicts political and civic apathy years later, we wanted to confirm that this result is valid. One of the biggest threats to our analysis is the possibility that there is something different about youths who get suspended versus those who do not get suspended, and that this difference is what really causes political apathy, not the suspension itself. If children who come from less stable families or who use drugs, for example, are more likely to be suspended and less likely to vote or volunteer, then our results might be misleading. We continued our analyses with an additional statistical technique designed to address this very problem: propensity score matching. We describe this in some detail in the appendix; let us just state here that we formed matched pairs of youths with very similar risk factors, but one member of each matched pair was suspended and one wasn't. This procedure resulted in exactly the same results, with suspended youths less likely to vote and volunteer years later.

Another possible complication is that our version of cause and effect is wrong. Given that suspension is so harmful to youths, perhaps being suspended causes negative behaviors like drug use and delinquency, and these behaviors are really the cause of civic and political apathy. We tested for this as well (see appendix) and found that this is not the case.

We checked, questioned, probed, and reconsidered our results in several ways to see if we could find an alternate explanation. We could not. In the end, we found that when children are suspended, they become adults who participate less in voting and community volunteering. And this is exactly what we had expected, based on previous research. Remember, as we discuss above: (1) while in school, children learn powerful lessons about how to behave as adults in society (this is the socialization process); and (2) school punishment teaches youths that they have no voice and no ability to challenge authority. It makes sense that the experience of being suspended has a lasting effect. Certainly, large numbers of youths do not internalize their suspensions in this way—but enough do that in the aggregate, the probability of voting and volunteering years later is influenced by suspension.

The differences shown in figure 6 may not look very large, but they are important. Considering all the many influences on whether someone votes and volunteers, and the many places where young people learn these behaviors (home, community, etc.), the fact that suspension on its own has such a robust influence on future behavior speaks volumes about the socializing influence of school punishment. Our purpose is not to show that suspension is the only influence, or even the most important influence on future behavior; instead we demonstrate that suspension in school has an effect that is both important and lasts years into the future.

Once again, this does not mean that nobody should be suspended for misbehavior in school. That would be ridiculous. Instead, our results show that the *overuse* of suspension is harmful. Typically, students are suspended for minor misbehaviors like talking back to a teacher or being generally disorderly and difficult, not for more harmful behaviors like fighting.[19] The number of youths suspended across the country has grown dramatically in recent years, despite the fact that school misbehavior has declined. This reliance on suspension—rather than efforts to help children improve their behavior—has costs years down the road, when those students have become adults who participate less in their communities.

Returning to Evelyn and her harsh commentary on the Mobile public schools, it is evident how schools communicate these antidemocratic messages. Later in her interview she describes how children are treated:

> Teachers and principals scream [at] a lot of students. Even if they're not talking to that student just . . . scream and holler at these children so much. Good God. And a lot of parents talk about this but we just don't do anything about it as a whole and that makes them nervous. It makes them not feel comfortable in that learning environment. It puts them in a box. [Students] are not able to defend themselves or address it if the teacher is saying something. They won't even give you time to say you didn't do it. Let's just say . . . [the teacher is] sending a message at her to be quiet shut up. In other words they want [students] to be like robots.

She discusses the very process we describe, in which authoritarian punishment and security can stifle student interaction and teach passivity.

This is very important for the health of democratic society. The overuse of suspension doesn't just harm the future life chances of the children who are suspended, or their families. The overuse of suspension harms all of us by discouraging citizens from participating in civic and political life. Democratic society works best when everyone participates, so that all views and needs can be represented. But if certain groups are discouraged from participating, then government represents only those who do participate, and not all of society. Returning to chapter 3, we also know that students of color are far more likely than White students to be disciplined in schools. When we consider the effects of suspension on future civic activity, this racial disproportionality in punishment takes on even graver significance. It is not only an issue of justice, but one of civic representation. Because they are more likely to be suspended, Black students are more likely to feel the brunt of undemocratic schooling. This can harm entire communities by suppressing volunteerism while weakening political representation through voter suppression. School suspension is thus an important mechanism for maintaining racial subordination in the United States.

Furthermore, widespread participation in community activities like volunteering is healthy because they increase our bonds to one another. Those who are suspended when young are less likely than others to enjoy these healthy experiences. The point is that suspension has ripple effects that may be subtle but that affect all of society—not just the students who are removed from school.

CONCLUSION

In this chapter we add another piece to the puzzle, demonstrating the long-term harms to everyone in society of our overuse of suspension. As I discussed in chapter 2, we can do better. It is indeed important to punish children when they break rules; otherwise the rules have little meaning. But we can punish them in ways that are more democratic and that do not socialize them into apathetic citizenship years later.

Consider, for example, the difference between restorative justice (see chapter 2) and suspension. Restorative justice practices include punishment, but they also require the offender to acknowledge how she has harmed the school community and the individual victim. Restorative justice treats an offending student as a valued member of the community who has made a mistake and is being held accountable. Compare that to suspension, which simply sends a student home, typically with little discussion or attempt to fix the problem. These students aren't treated like valued members of a community; they're treated like problems who need to go away. It shouldn't be surprising that at least some of these youths internalize that message and allow it to shape their behavior years later.

7 Financial Costs of School Security and Punishment

The issue of school safety tends to arouse fear and impassioned responses. Discussions of how best to respond to these fears often meet standard partisan scripts: conservatives may be more likely to endorse the type of heavy police presence with strict accountability measures that have become common since the 1990s, while liberals may prefer alternative responses like restorative justice. In an attempt to move the conversation forward on common ground, this chapter is focused on something that speaks to everyone's interests: saving money.

Unlike almost any other governmental action, for some reason we don't often speak about how much it costs to police and punish students. Consider, for example, the massive debate about the finances of health care reform surrounding the 2010 Affordable Care Act (aka Obamacare); our discussion about whether individuals ought to receive assistance with life-saving medical care is mired in arguments about money, yet it is difficult to find any discussion in the public arena of how much it costs to put surveillance cameras in schools.

As it turns out, our current school security and punishment practices are expensive. While this probably isn't surprising, given how much we spend on education overall, it is certainly an issue that needs to be considered in detail. As discussed in other chapters, the evidence tells us that a lot of what we currently do to keep schools safe is ineffective at best, and harmful in several ways. How much do these ineffective, potentially harmful practices cost us?

CURRENT DIRECT COSTS

To begin thinking about the costs of school security and punishment, I want to work through what it costs a school to have the related equipment and personnel. Certainly, schools differ in what personnel they hire and what equipment they have. Yet an image of a typical school—particularly a typical high school—emerges: while relatively few schools have metal detectors, for example, most public high schools have a daily presence of armed police or security guards (63.3 percent),[1] security cameras (81.2 percent), and locked or monitored doors (83.9 percent).[2]

To understand how much schools spend on security and punishment, I spoke to the chief financial officer of a school district in my own state, Delaware, who went through his books and told me how much his district spends on school safety. The district is fairly high-performing academically and is not known for having particular problems with student misbehavior. About 40 percent of the students in the district are classified by the district as "low income"; about 50 percent of the student body is White non-Hispanic, and about one-third is African American. The district has a mix of students but is known locally as a preferred district for enrolling one's children, and as a district without a publicly visible student behavior problem. While this is just one district, the costs that I discuss below are all for practices, personnel, or equipment that are very common across the United States. I list these costs in table 1.

Several items are easy to calculate, such as the costs of the service contracts the district has with companies that oversee their security cameras and provide staff members called "interventionists," who intervene in student misbehavior cases. Other costs, such as the salaries of the deans of students, are easy to calculate but hard to interpret. A dean of students spends much of her time responding to student misbehavior and deciding on punishment—but she also does other things within the school. In table 1, assuming

Table 1   Local District Security and Discipline Costs in Dollars

A. Personnel	Average salary	Number employed	Percentage of time on school safety	Annual cost
School resource officers (SROs)	72,500	4	100	290,000
Overhead—SROs (25% of salary)				72,500
Deans of students	100,000	8	67	536,000
Overhead—Deans (25% of salary)				134,000

B. Alternative programs	Total cost		Percentage of program involving therapeutic services (subtracted)	Annual cost
Alternative to suspension program	1,300,000		25	975,000

C. Service contracts				Annual cost
Interventionists				472,000
Surveillance camera monitoring				212,500

D. Equipment	Cost per school	Number of schools	Total cost	Annual cost
Walkie-talkies			120,000	8,000
Front doors	170,000	15	2,550,000	170,000
Entrance video system	25,000	15	375,000	25,000
Card entrance system	80,000	15	1,200,000	80,000
Surveillance cameras	24,000	15	360,000	24,000

E. Maintenance	Annual cost per school	Number of schools	Annual cost
Front doors	5,000	15	75,000
Security software	4,000	15	60,000
Other tech maintenance	8,000	15	120,000

Total estimated annual costs 3,254,000

that these deans spend about two-thirds of their time directly on student punishment, I include only this portion of their salaries. I also include 25 percent of the salaries of school resource officers (SROs) and deans of students to account for overhead (fringe benefits, insurance, and employer taxes). Other costs involve one-time expenses such as the cost of building secure front doors (doors that lock, have an intercom for visitors to request access, and would be difficult to break down) or installing surveillance cameras. To be conservative, I assume that these systems need to be replaced every fifteen years. Given all the assumptions that I needed to make to put these numbers together, they should certainly be interpreted with caution. But they are helpful, since they offer us a starting point for discussing the financial cost of discipline and security.

Table 1 lists only the school district's expenses for personnel, programs, contracts, and equipment related to school security and punishment. One of these items is a $1.3 million alternative-to-suspension program where students can go if they are removed from school, without being suspended out of school. This program provides therapeutic services such as credit recovery, counseling, and family engagement, which are very different from the other security- and punishment-oriented costs listed. To subtract the cost of these services from the estimated security and punishment costs, I estimate that about 25 percent of this program's costs go to these therapeutic services, and thus include only 75 percent of the total program cost in my count of security and discipline costs. Other students who are suspended long term are indeed removed from school. These youths go to alternative schools, and the state pays this tab. The district's assistant superintendent estimated that the state pays about $1.7 million for alternative school provisions for students in this district.

By my estimate, this district spends over $3.25 million a year on school security and punishment. There are about 11,000 students in the district,[3] and the district spends almost $13,000 per student annually; of this, by my calculations, about $300 per student is spent on security and punishment per year. This may be a relatively small portion of the schools' overall budgets, but it's a large amount of money nonetheless. If this figure were cut in half, for example, the district would have an extra $1.6 million to spend on hiring teachers or enhancing the curriculum, or on implementing practices that have a better chance of maintaining safety, such as additional school counselors, restorative justice programs, tutors, and so on (see chapter 2). When considering these costs, it is important to remember that this is a high-performing district that is sought out for its academic excellence, and one with fairly typical security and punishment practices.

If we think about this figure on a national scale, the expense is eye-popping. According to the National Center for Education Statistics, there were 49,256,120 students enrolled in public schools in the United States in 2011–12.[4] If schools across the United States spent, on average, $300 per pupil on school safety expenses, this would total almost $14.8 billion.

> Estimated national annual direct cost of school safety practices: $14.8 billion

In my own school district—where I send my children to public schools and for which I pay taxes—there was recently an operating tax referendum up for vote (it was approved). The article describing the referendum that appeared in the district's newsletter (sent to all residents within the district) states that "Funding allocated in the referendum allows the district to continue a number of high-priority initiatives and improvements outlined in the 2013 Strategic Plan. They include increased security measures and school resource officers, reading specialists, after school programs, infrastructure improvements such as playgrounds and technology, curriculum program such as STEM and International Baccalaureate and alternative placement programs."[5] Security measures and SROs are the first items listed as "high-priority initiatives" for which more money is needed.

Clearly, school security and punishment are expensive. Yet these expenses are rarely discussed—instead they are just assumed to be necessary. As we saw in chapter 2, this is not necessarily the case. Some of them are very sensible, such as having securely locked front doors, but others do not seem to achieve much benefit, according to the evaluation research.

We also need to think about how these expenses vary across schools. In earlier research, Geoff Ward and I found that schools with larger proportions of poor students and students of color are more likely than schools with mostly middle-class White students to have metal detectors, use drug-sniffing police dogs, and hire SROs or security guards. These differences are most pronounced among elementary and middle schools.[6] Meanwhile, schools that serve poor students and mostly students of color tend to receive less funding than others. These school districts tend to have lower tax bases, and often receive less funding from their states as well, yet they tend to be in greater disrepair and host students who require more social services.[7] This means that the schools with the greatest deficits and needs, and with the lowest levels of funding, also tend to have the most expensive security practices. Compared to such districts, the one whose finances I discuss here is well off: just over 50 percent of students in the district are White, about 44 percent are classified as "low income," and the district has almost $13,000 to spend per pupil per year. It can better afford some of these practices than an inner-city district with greater need, less money, yet more security infrastructure.

LOSS OF INCOME

In addition to direct costs, we also need to consider how much money schools fail to receive because of school punishment. School funding is very complex and varies considerably across states. But funding, particularly how much money a state gives to any school, is based on a formula that includes the number of students enrolled. Students who are suspended long term, enrolled in alternative placements, or expelled may not be counted in the school's enrollment, and thus they may be excluded from the counts used to determine a school's funding.

Whether or not school suspension results in loss of income depends on how a school or district counts their enrollment. In Delaware, it seems unlikely that suspension has a significant effect on funding in this way. According to Delaware state regulations,[8] for the purpose of funding, school enrollment is based on the number of students enrolled at the end of September. Students who are enrolled but absent on any particular day are counted, so long as they are absent for a medical reason or absent for fewer than ten days. Students who are expelled or suspended long term and sent to alternative schools are counted as still enrolled in the original school. Students in detention facilities are included, but only if they will return to school before November 1. The only way that school punishment can reduce enrollment directly is if a student is suspended for at least ten days at the end of September, or if school misbehavior results in their incarceration. While I cannot verify how many youths this applies to (these data are unavailable), it is not likely to be very many; most suspensions are for less than ten days (otherwise they receive alternative provisions), and relatively few students from any school are in long-term detention.

However, in other jurisdictions, school punishment can be a significant reason for lost revenue. Consider the following statement, from the Council for State Government's influential "School Discipline Consensus Report":

> Lower attendance rates due to suspension and expulsion also impact school and district funding because they are tied to state assistance dollars based on Average Daily Attendance (ADA). Under the conservative assumption that every out-of-school suspension represents an absence of 1.5 days, the San Antonio Independent School District lost almost a half a million dollars in state revenue in the 2010–11 school year. In the Fresno Unified School District, students in a single year missed 32,180 days of school due to suspensions, costing the district more than one million dollars in lost state revenue that is based on students' ADA.[9]

Of course, it may be a worthwhile investment for schools to remove some students even if they must forgo some funding to do so. Some students cost more than others in terms of using resources—particularly staff time and energy—so the school may be financially better off if more difficult students are removed, even if this means that income leaves with them. But is this what we want, and is this how we want schools to make decisions? Democratic ideals hold that all students are *entitled* to a public education, even the difficult ones.

RELATED FUTURE COSTS

The growth in school suspensions that we have observed across the United States comes with substantial long-term costs. In immediate costs, suspension is far less expensive than other interventions—the school spends nothing to remove a student, other than the possibility of lost income. But the long-term costs of removing students from school are far from trivial. As many studies have conclusively shown, students who are suspended or expelled are at increased risk of dropping out and of involvement in the justice system, both of which bear many costs to society. Any discussion of the consequences of school security and punishment must address these costs.

Dropping Out

School punishment can influence future employment prospects, but only indirectly. Future employers will not know whether someone was suspended in school (school records may be permanent, but they aren't accessible to potential employers), so school punishment on its own has no direct effect. Instead, punishment shapes some outcomes, such as the likelihood of graduation or of involvement with the juvenile justice system, which in turn influence future employment. Since I discuss the justice system's involvement in the next section, let me focus here only on the likelihood of graduation and future employment.

Research on youths who are punished in school has very clearly shown that kids who are suspended are more likely than others to be held back a grade or to drop out of high school. For example, the authors of the landmark Texas report "Breaking Schools' Rules" find that youths who are suspended are significantly more likely than others to repeat a grade or drop out.[10] In subsequent analyses of these data, Marchbanks et al. find that students who experience 1.4 disciplinary events per year (this is the average number of school punishments, for those who received any) have twice the probability of repeating a grade compared to those with no disciplinary events. Given the size of the Texas school system, this translates into an additional 5,432 students each year who repeat a grade; they require an additional year of schooling and thus consume an additional year of resources. Marchbanks et al. calculate the price tag of these additional students at $63 million per year for the state of Texas.[11]

Marchbanks et al. continue by considering the problem of dropping out. They find that students who are disciplined 1.4 times per year (the average number of disciplinary incidents) are 29 percent more likely to drop out than others. They write: "If the 59% of students who are disciplined dropped out at rates comparable to their peers who avoided punishment, the overall dropout rate in Texas would be approximately 13% lower."[12] Marchbanks et al. turn to a prior analysis, also in Texas, of how much dropouts cost the state.[13] The analysis includes costs such as lost wages to the individuals who drop out, lost sales-tax revenue to the state, welfare costs associated with high school dropouts, and increased criminal justice costs. This analysis finds that dropouts in Texas from the high school class of 2012 alone cost the state somewhere between $5.4 billion (using very conservative estimates) and $6.9 billion (using less conservative estimates). Marchbanks et al. apply this to the issue of school punishment by assuming that school punishment is responsible for about 13 percent of the dropout rate: "If the state were able to reduce the effects of discipline on likelihood of dropping out by 13%, the level associated with school discipline, the total savings would be between $711 million and $1.3 billion."[14]

Other scholars have also found that children who are suspended or punished in other ways at school are at increased risk of dropping out. For example, prominent education researcher Robert Balfanz and colleagues find that each suspension in ninth grade is associated with a 20 percent decrease of one's odds of graduating.[15] In another recent study, Talisha Lee and colleagues analyze data from hundreds of schools in Virginia and find that a school's suspension rate statistically explains 10 percent of a school's dropout rate—after accounting for important factors such as race/ethnicity, poverty, expenditure per pupil, location (urbanicity), students' attitudes, and students' belief in school rules.[16] This is helpful because it allows us to extrapolate in broader terms to students (and former students) across the country, connecting the costs of the national dropout rate to school suspension.

Counts of dropout rates vary, since some estimates assume that anyone who takes longer than four years to complete high school is a dropout. But according to more conservative estimates that are used by the National Center for Education Statistics, in 2012 there were 2,562,000 people in the United States between the ages of sixteen and twenty-four who were not in school and did not have a GED or high school diploma. If we assume, as a low estimate, that school suspensions are responsible for 10 percent of this (as in Lee et al.'s study), and, as a high estimate, 13 percent (as in Marchbanks et al.'s study), then school punishment is responsible for between 256,200 and 333,060 dropouts (ages sixteen to twenty-four) across the United States. If we assume that each dropout costs an annual average of $4,935 (as calculated in Texas, considering lost income, lost sales-tax revenue, welfare payments, and criminal-justice-system costs),[17] then the national population of sixteen- to twenty-four-year old dropouts that is attributable to school punishment costs us somewhere between $1.26 billion and $1.64 billion. But again, this is the cost *each year* and includes only dropouts in this age range. Further, the annual cost per dropout is estimated on the basis of data in Texas, which has the twenty-sixth highest median income[18] and welfare payments that are considerably below the national average;[19] thus, the financial cost is likely even higher in other states.

> Dropout estimate 1—National annual cost of additional dropouts (ages sixteen to twenty-four): $1.26 billion to $1.64 billion

In 2011 the Alliance for Excellent Education conducted a similar analysis, but nationwide. Their report considered the difference in unemployment and average earning between those with and without high school diplomas and found that a single year's worth of dropouts cost the national economy $154 billion.[20] If we again assume that 10 to 13 percent of dropouts are the result of school discipline, then we wind up with a figure that is far higher than the one based on the Texas research: between $15.4 billion and $20.0 billion. And these figures consider only the effect of lost wages, not peripheral costs such as additional welfare payments and increased criminal justice costs.

> Dropout estimate 2—National annual cost of additional dropouts: $15.4 billion to $20.0 billion

Juvenile Justice System Involvement

Another indirect expense of school punishment is the cost of involvement in the juvenile justice system. As discussed in chapter 2, there is solid evidence that the presence of SROs results in increased arrests of students for trivial offenses. Given the alternative options for responding to minor offenses such as fighting and being disorderly—including counseling, anger management programs, mentoring, and so on—this is unfortunate. In addition to the substantial harms these youths and their families face by being subjected to unnecessary justice system involvement, it is expensive!

A recent study by the Justice Policy Institute finds that in thirty-three states, juvenile incarceration can cost over $100,000 per year; the national average price tag for incarcerating a juvenile is $88,000 per year.[21] Because they require more attention, care, services, and protection than adults do, juveniles are more expensive to incarcerate than adults. Of course, only a small percentage—7.8 percent, according to national data— of juveniles that are arrested and referred to the juvenile justice system wind up "placed" in a residential facility (this is the juvenile justice system's euphemism for sentencing a youth to incarceration).[22] And when they are incarcerated, most youths serve substantially less than a year in a residential facility, most commonly 91–180 days.[23]

Even if youths are not incarcerated, any justice system involvement they experience is costly. Court processing requires the time of prosecutors, a judge, a court clerk, and security staff. It also requires defense attorneys, many of whom (particularly in urban areas)[24] are paid by the state because the defendants cannot afford them. In addition to these professionals' time, there are costs associated with the maintenance and operation of sometimes lavish court buildings.

It is difficult to estimate how many youths are referred to the juvenile justice system because of school safety practices. This is because any reasonable estimate has to consider the youths that are referred there, above and beyond the number that would have been referred had the school not had an SRO or other security and punishment practices.

Again, because it is so comprehensive and conducted over many years, I find the Texas study "Breaking Schools' Rules" a helpful resource for making estimates. The authors of this study find that suspension or expulsion for a discretionary offense resulted in a 2.85 times greater likelihood of contact with the juvenile justice system. It is important that the researchers considered only discretionary offenses here—this excludes youths who are punished for more serious infractions, since these youths are likely to be involved in the justice system only because of their behavior, with no push from the school. The authors estimate that about 17,000 students per grade cohort are referred to the juvenile justice system in Texas because of school suspension and expulsion.[25] This is above and beyond the number that would otherwise have been arrested and referred to court.

If we use the national rate of incarceration among those referred to juvenile court (7.8 percent) and apply it to the Texas estimate, 1,326 additional youths (7.8 percent of 17,000 students) are incarcerated per school-year cohort in Texas. Again using national norms, if these 1,326 youths serve an average of 135 days,[26] at a price tag of $88,000 per year (the average, as reported by the Justice Policy Institute), their incarceration costs Texas $43.1 million. While it is true that juvenile incarceration rates have been decreasing since 1995,[27] it seems that the incarceration rate has room to drop even further if not kept unnecessarily high by excessive school security and punishment.

Another recent study might prove even more helpful in estimating the costs of school-based arrests for minor offenses. Criminologists Chongmin Na and Denise C. Gottfredson analyzed nationally representative data collected by the U.S. Department of Education to understand the effects of police officers in schools (i.e., SROs). They find that schools with SROs refer a much larger percentage of minor offenses to law enforcement than schools without SROs. This is particularly true for the most common crime that students commit in schools: simple assault without a weapon. In fact, schools with SROs refer *twice* as many of these offenses to the juvenile justice system as other schools.[28] Certainly, much of this result is due to the fact that schools with SROs may be more dangerous or disorderly to begin with; but when the researchers account for these factors and consider the impact of adding one more SRO to a school, they find that the rate of referring nonserious violent crime to the justice system increases 12.3 percent when schools add an SRO to their staff.

In addition to providing concrete evidence about the relationship between police presence in schools and additional juvenile referrals to court, this study is helpful for pointing out the importance of scrutinizing minor offenses, and simple assault in particular. As I have discussed in my earlier work, it is common now in some schools for minor fistfights—which are unfortunate but common, and have always been common—to result in arrest, even when nobody is hurt.[29] We can look at national juvenile court statistics to consider the influence nationally of SROs on simple-assault arrest rates specifically.

In figure 7, I graph the number of aggravated assault cases and simple assault cases referred to juvenile courts, nationwide.[30] I also include a third line, which is the number of aggravated assault cases times five. Since there are many more simple assault cases than aggravated assault cases, putting the two on one graph makes it difficult to see the trend for aggravated assault (its scale is so low); multiplying it by five allows the trend (not the numbers of cases in any given year) to be compared to that of simple assault.

This figure tells an interesting and important story. From the 1980s to the mid-1990s, juvenile crime—particularly violence—rose steeply. But juvenile violence then began to decline in the mid-1990s. This trend is displayed by aggravated assault cases: there were just over half as many aggravated assault referrals in 2011 as in the peak year, 1995. This is certainly not the case for simple assault—the number of simple assault referrals in 2011 is roughly the same as that in 1994, near the peak of the juvenile violence epidemic seen in the '90s, and more than double the number from 1985. The trend of simple assault cases suggests that young people today are more likely than those in years past to be arrested for simple assault, even when all other indicators of juvenile crime are going down.

Looking again at figure 7, the period between 1995 and 2006 is particularly interesting: aggravated assault cases show a steep decline for most of this period (after a steep decline, cases crept up during 2002–06), while simple assault cases continued to rise. This time frame coincides with the significant buildup of SROs in schools nationwide. While many other factors might cause simple-assault arrest rates to be high, it is reasonable to speculate that the presence of SROs is responsible for at least part of this trend. As Na and Gottfredson and other researchers have shown, the presence of SROs does result in increased rates of arrest for nonserious violence, particularly simple assault. It makes sense that the effect is observed for minor offenses like simple assault, given that a more serious offense (e.g., aggravated assault) at school will likely result in a justice system referral, regardless of whether an SRO is on site.

Imagine an alternative scenario. Imagine that the trend in simple assault referrals still mirrored the trend in aggravated assault referrals, just

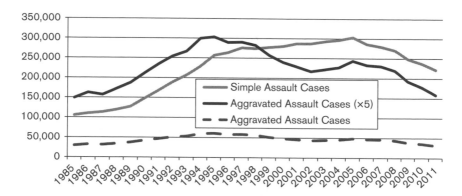

Figure 7. Numbers of youths referred to juvenile court for simple assault and aggravated assault, nationwide, 1985–2011. Also shown, for better comparison, are the aggravated-assault numbers multiplied by five. Source: Melissa Sickmund et al. (2014) "Easy access to juvenile court statistics: 1985–2011" (accessed online at www. ojjdp.gov/ojstatbb/ezajcs/).

as it did until 1995. In this case, we would see that simple assaults would have declined much more than they did after 1995, so that the number of cases in 2011 would be comparable to the number in 1985. If this were the case, there would have been 116,000 fewer referrals for simple assault in 2011, and 6,200 fewer youths incarcerated for simple assault.[31] Using the same estimates I used above (average of 135 days incarcerated, at a cost of $88,000 per year), this results in a cost of $201.7 million.

> Estimated national annual cost of additional youths incarcerated for simple assault: $201.7 million

Limitations in Financial Estimates

At this point, many readers are probably doubting the accuracy or usefulness of some of these estimates. Certainly, there are limitations to this exercise of estimating the financial cost of school security and discipline. But as I describe below, this is an important piece for understanding all costs and consequences of our current practices, so that we can have a more informed discussion about the best path forward.

One clear limitation to my analyses in this chapter is that I have only considered the costs, and none of the benefits, of security and suspension. As discussed at length in chapter 2, it is certainly necessary for schools to have fair, firm, and consistently enforced rules. At no point have I suggested that there should be no security, or that student misbehavior should go unpunished. In fact, some research suggests that students who attend schools with strict rules are more likely to graduate and maintain employment years later.[32] But as I have discussed at length in this book, the issue is how these policies are enforced and whether we address students' underlying issues. The evidence is clear that we suspend and police youths more than necessary, with harmful consequences. It is entirely a false pretense to assume that students must either be suspended or have their misbehavior ignored, since there are so many other options that would be less costly (in the long run) and show better student outcomes.

While suspension at some level is necessary, as is some security cost, my intent in this chapter is to consider the *surplus* of security and discipline that exists in many schools across the United States. When discussing direct costs of security, I consider how much money we could save if we were to cut our security practices and personnel in half, not eliminate them altogether. When looking at the consequences of suspension on dropping out, I isolate the portion of dropouts that I estimate to be due to school punishment alone and not to other factors that might more reasonably motivate one to drop out, such as the need to support a family, school failure, and so on. And when analyzing the link between school punishment and juvenile court referral, I consider both the portion of arrests attributable to school punishment and the change in court referrals over time that coincides with the buildup of SROs in schools. The issue is not whether we have strict punishments or how firm the school rules are. Instead the issue is the cost to students, schools, and taxpayers of importing more security personnel, equipment, and practices than are necessary, and of using harsh school punishment as a first rather than a last resort. In other words, my analyses already assume that some security and punishment are crucial, but that too much is harmful.

That said, there is one cost saving that comes from school punishment: students who drop out because of school punishment save the school money. Yet the analyses by Alvarez et al., on which the estimates of how much each dropout in Texas costs, already calculated this cost saving and included it in the final tally I used above.

Another limitation to my analyses is how many assumptions they require. I have assumed that a dean of students spends two-thirds of her time on school discipline, that a front door needs to be replaced every fifteen years, that the Texas estimates of the cost of dropout apply elsewhere, and so on. This is problematic, no doubt about it. But in making these assumptions I have erred on the side of being conservative, so as not to inflate the cost of school security and discipline unnecessarily. Hopefully, most of my assumptions are near correct—but what if they aren't? What if I am way off, say 50 percent off? Would it change anything to estimate that school punishment's contribution to the social costs of dropouts is only $600–800 million (instead of $1.26–1.64 billion, using the much lower of the two estimates I discussed above)? It seems to me that it's like asking whether it changes much if one is pilfered of $5,000 or $10,000— both are dreadful. Stated differently, would we be OK with wasting only $600 million of precious school funds, given all that we want schools to achieve, so long as it's not $1.2 billion? I doubt it.

Similarly, one could argue that even if my assumptions are correct, reality is far more complex than these estimates allow. For example, does school suspension result in justice system involvement, or do kids who get arrested later get suspended from school?[33] If a school does not hire an SRO, doesn't the same municipality pay that same police officer's salary, except that then it comes out of the police department's budget instead of the school's? Perhaps more importantly, is it fair to count costs as if they mean money is lost, going nowhere and to nobody? The money spent on incarceration, for example, goes toward individual correctional officers' salaries and back into the economy; the assumption of lost wages presumes that had that individual continued her education, a willing employer would have had a job for her to take; and so on.

The point of all of these analyses isn't to nail down a specific dollar amount that identifies the true cost of school security and punishment. Instead it's to point out that our current practices carry a very large price tag, one that is dreadful even if my assumptions and estimates are somewhat inflated. Conversations about how we maintain school safety very rarely address these costs or even acknowledge their existence. This is a costly oversight.

In his book *Punished: Policing the Lives of Black and Latino Boys,* sociologist Victor M. Rios[34] disagrees with the often mentioned claim of progressives that society has abandoned social spending on the most disadvantaged, particularly inner-city youths of color. He vividly illustrates that we spend a great deal of money on these youths—but these resources go to intensive policing and punishment, not to social welfare spending. That is, governments invest heavily in added police presence, court staff, probation officers, correctional facilities, and other branches of punishment and policing, while underfunding social welfare programs that might help some of these youths avoid the criminal justice system. With regard to school security and discipline, I find Rios's argument to ring true. This is especially true when one considers that youths of color are more likely to attend schools with more intensive security and punishment.[35] Schools— especially schools serving youths with the greatest needs—spend scarce resources on expensive security and punishment practices that offer little by way of crime prevention while doing harm to students, schools, and families. Public funds that could be spent on public education for those who most need it are instead spent on security and punishment, draining public coffers while supporting growing private security industries.[36] Rather than spending on school infrastructure, academic enrichment, student counselors, or other supports for students and teachers, these funds pay for services provided by private companies, such as the $212,500 per year in the district near me that goes to a company to monitor security cameras (see table 1).

As a final note on the costs of school safety efforts, I want to return to a theme I discussed earlier in this book: the damaging effect of unnecessary school security and punishment on innovation and productivity. In this chapter, I have estimated how much schools pay for security and punishment practices, as well as the costs of incarceration and lost wages. But I haven't even begun to estimate the costs incurred when large numbers of young people who might be future innovators and leaders are diverted from this path rather than being encouraged to contribute, socially and economically, to society.

8 Conclusion

In the aftermath of horrific tragedies such as the attack in Newtown, Connecticut, we are all scared and looking for answers to a very important question: How can we best keep children safe at school? This book has considered what we do in the name of preventing school crime and disorder, what effects our actions have, and what we can do better.

The real school safety problem is not that we have too many out-of-control kids, overly lenient school discipline, or too few police in schools. Instead, the real problem is that school security and punishment are too punitive and rigid: we rely too much on policing, suspension, and expulsion instead of helping kids solve their problems and properly caring for them. As I summarized in chapter 2, researchers have documented several harms that come from what we do: growing racial inequality, increased dropout rates, deterioration of the school social climate, and arrest histories for individual youths.

In the preceding chapters, I added new pieces to the discussion by focusing on harms of excessive security and punishment that have not previously been considered. I have demonstrated how school suspension can hurt entire families and reduce future civic participation, and how unfair rules can teach bullying behavior to kids. I have also pointed out the high, often hidden financial costs of school security and punishment. In an era of school funding crises, it seems odd that the finances of school security and punishment have not drawn much attention before now.

Nothing I have written suggests that rules or punishments are unimportant, or that student misbehavior should be ignored. This would be a complete misinterpretation of the evidence. Instead, it is now very clear that we have gone too far. School rules and punishments must be firm and fair, but reasonable. Many schools across the United States, having lost this sense of reason, are punishing and policing too much.

PRINCIPLES FOR MOVING FORWARD

Thankfully, the large body of evidence on school safety is not all negative—there is a good deal of research on effective practices as well, which I discussed in chapter 2. While there are several specific programs that schools could implement—perhaps the most common is Positive Behavioral Intervention and Supports—schools could instead choose a more basic path forward. The following are seven key principles for how schools can reimagine ways to interact with children, each of which has great promise and evidence supporting it as effective.

1. Don't assume the worst. Children tend to respond to expectations, be they good or bad. If we assume that they are either criminals or potential criminals, the chances are decent that many of them will fulfill these expectations. But if we instead show them trust and confidence, and allow them the opportunity to show us how good they can be, they will often live up to these better expectations. Certainly, they will sometimes let us down, which is OK—as adults, we can live with the disappointment and know that high expectations are more likely to produce good outcomes than bad ones, even if letting our guard down sometimes comes at a cost. It is sadly ironic that our buildup of security and punishment—the embodiment of an assumption that children are out of control—has come at the same time that children have become so much better behaved in schools (and elsewhere).

2. Stop doing unnecessary harm. Sometimes arrest, suspension, and expulsion are necessary in order to protect others in the school or to allow teachers to do their jobs. But the evidence shows that we rely on punishment and arrest more than necessary, particularly for youths of color and in response to minor forms of misbehavior such as disrespecting teachers or causing a disturbance in the hallway. This overreliance is harmful to students, schools, families, and communities. We need to be more restrained when we choose to punish or arrest students, recognizing that these practices are very costly and should be used only when other options are unavailable or insufficient. Consider, for example, the agreements brokered by Steven C. Teske and J. Brian Huff that I discussed in chapter 2; these judges recognized that arrest and suspension need to be used more sparingly, and they helped school resource officers (SROs) and school staff find less severe—and more effective—alternatives. Jurisdictions across the country should follow their model by agreeing that minor misbehaviors such as cursing or disrespect to staff do not need to result in suspension or arrest.

3. Help solve problems. The biggest failure of most school punishment is that it fails to help anyone—the child, teacher, or school. When we choose to kick kids out of class or out of school without addressing the causes of their misbehavior, we miss an opportunity to prevent reoccurrence of the problem. It can be time consuming and frustrating to sit down and talk to a disrespectful, disruptive child, but it can prevent problems in the future. During my research, I met some teachers who are wonderful at this. They take the time and spend the energy talking to kids and getting to the source of the problems; they are rewarded with more respectful and engaged students who behave better. Doing this requires skill, charisma, and a rapport with children. It requires empathy, patience, and understanding. Not many of us are able to develop these skills without a great deal of practice. We need to equip teachers and other school staff with the training, support, and time needed to practice these behaviors, so that they can address children's problems rather than only removing these children from their classes. This means talking to a disruptive child, one-on-one, in a caring manner and investing energy in supporting that child. Certainly, it is necessary to remove them from class or school sometimes, but the teacher's and school's job should not end there—they should continue to try to remedy whatever caused the misbehavior.

4. Allow for redemption. When it is necessary to remove students, via suspension or arrest, it is important to more carefully monitor their return to school. Students who are removed from school must be given a chance to redeem themselves and to reintegrate into the community as full members, not outcasts. This shows compassion and caring and allows the student and others to see him or her as a member of the school community rather than as a bad kid. This is what effective parents do—they punish when necessary, but allow the child to maintain status as a loved member of the family.

5. Empower kids. As we know, schools with inclusive social climates tend to have lower rates of student misbehavior than other schools. In addition to establishing fair and reasonable rules and punishments, and facilitating bonds between students and teachers, schools can help establish inclusive climates by deliberately empowering children to participate in school governance. Student government should not just be lip service or limited to planning school dances—students should be involved in running the school overall. Adults still need to have the final say on what the rules are and how they are enforced, but in most schools there is a lot of room for increasing students' stake in how the school is run. This might be done through greater student representation in forming school rules; peer court tribunals that decide on other students' punishments; peer mentoring; or other strategies. These practices would empower kids to behave better by helping them feel like wanted parts of the school rather than nuisances.

6. Empower teachers. Much of the discussion about any school reform seems to assume that teachers have unlimited energy and will to take on whatever new task politicians think they ought to do. But like students, teachers get frustrated. We need to more carefully and respectfully train and support teachers to punish students more effectively. If school discipline reform is pushed on teachers as yet another demand, or interpreted by them as an assumption that they have failed, then the reform is destined to go poorly. But if reform is instead done in a way that recognizes the commitment and care to children that most teachers show, and if it makes their jobs easier rather than adding to their already difficult workloads, then it has a greater chance of success. This requires resources: paid time for training in how to de-escalate conflict with a student, additional support staff who can help talk to disruptive students, and even smaller classes (so that teachers can better build rapport with individual students). Teachers who feel supported and empowered are likely to pass that on to their students than a teacher who feels frustrated and has little patience or empathy for a struggling child.

7. *Empower parents.* The stories reported in chapter 4 show parents who tried to interact with schools on their children's behalf and felt shut out. While we only heard half of the story—the parents' versions only—it is clear that these schools could have done more to make parents feel welcomed and listened to. Parents who are able to work with the school can help reinforce the school's message at home by encouraging their children to behave while at school. But parents must be part of the team that addresses the issue, not silent bystanders. Certainly, some of the problem with parental participation resides in parents who do not wish to get involved. But schools could take steps to recognize the limitations some parents face (e.g., work schedules, being intimidated) and empower them to participate more. School staff need to understand that many parents— particularly working-class parents—may be uninvolved because they trust the school to do its job, or because they feel out of place there, but not because they don't care about their children.[1] School staff need to proactively reach out to these parents to help them feel welcomed and important, and this should occur before there is a problem to discuss, so that their first interaction is positive rather than negative.

Each of these principles borrows from effective parenting techniques. They show respect and compassion; they seek to establish order with as little harm as possible; they attempt to solve problems and teach children how to behave better; and they help adults rather than make their jobs more difficult.

OBSTACLES TO REFORM

In just the past few years, there has been substantial movement toward reforming school security and punishment in the direction that I have advocated. In 2014 alone, cities like Oakland, Los Angeles, San Francisco, Columbus, Chicago, and Philadelphia all passed school discipline or security reform. Some states, including Colorado in 2012 and California in 2013, have as well. Even the federal government has been involved in this issue; in January 2014, for example, the Department of Justice and Department of Education released a joint "Dear Colleague" letter, with a series of informational resources for schools, that encouraged the use of restorative punishments and efforts to build school social climates, while limiting the use of arrest and suspensions in schools.

This trend is impressive and is exactly what one would hope, since it follows from the evidence on how to best maintain school safety. It suggests that the tide may be turning, that punitive school discipline and rigid security may be falling out of favor among policy-makers. But I'm not convinced that these reforms will result in the real changes we need in order to fix our real school safety problem. These policy reforms sound good, but there are several obstacles that I fear will get in the way of their having a meaningful impact across the country.

Budgetary Constraints

Clearly, one important obstacle to reinventing school safety efforts is a lack of money. Schools nationwide are strapped for cash, even as we have now come out of the Great Recession. Efforts to tutor children (who act up in class because they do not understand course material), to train staff in running restorative justice sessions, and to counsel students take money. Additional staff or staff training are required for many of these efforts. To implement some (e.g., tutoring), teachers may need to work additional hours, which is unlikely to be approved by teachers' unions without significant compensation.

The evidence strongly suggests that these practices would save money in the long run by reducing student misbehavior and allowing teachers to focus more on teaching. This might allow schools to redirect money away from expensive security and punishment practices, and toward student supports or direct instruction. As chapter 7 made clear, with fewer dropouts and fewer juveniles arrested—both of which result from our current policing and punishment strategies—taxpayers would save a great deal of money.

But long-run savings do not mean we have the money to fully implement these plans today. With school budgets the way they are, it is difficult to imagine much change in terms of new personnel, training, or programs in many schools across the country. Maintaining the status quo regarding personnel and staff training will make it very difficult for real change in school disciplinary practice to take hold.

Existing Demands on Teachers

I do not envy public school teachers, given how much they must constantly deal with. They receive insufficient resources to do an extremely difficult job. This job includes teaching academic subjects as well as preparing students for standardized tests and teaching children how to be citizens. Not surprisingly, the job of teacher occasionally makes some "most stressful job" lists.[2] Yes, they have summers off. But the demands of teaching so many students—with relatively little time for lesson preparation, and having to manage difficult students' behavior—more than makes up for that benefit, in my opinion.

And yet, as hard as teachers work, the majority of Americans perceive them to be failing. The public is typically discouraged with the state of education in the United States and wants to see improvement; for example, a 2012 Gallup poll found that only 29 percent of Americans expressed confidence in public schools—the lowest score on this question since Gallup began asking it in 1973.[3] There have also been challenges to tenure for teachers, which may indicate public impatience with teachers, or assumptions that too many teachers take advantage of the system. As examples, consider the following: the movie *Waiting for Superman*, which forcefully argued against teacher tenure and highlighted the problem of ineffective teachers; reformers like Washington, D.C., Schools Chancellor Michelle Rhee, who dismissed hundreds of teachers during 2007–10;[4] or a 2014 California court decision that ruled teacher tenure unconstitutional.[5] Each of these examples was a direct attack on teachers, since each clearly communicated impatience with ineffective teachers, as well as the beliefs that such teachers are commonplace and that tenure foolishly protects them from accountability.

Clearly, large segments of the American public hold negative views about teachers and schools. Our response is to demand change, and for the federal government to impose new standards and regulations. In the past fifteen years, this has come in the form of massive federal policy reforms—including No Child Left Behind, Race to the Top, and Common Core Standards. With each new policy reform, we ask schools to shift how they teach. This requires new curricula, new training, new approaches, new textbooks, and thus new headaches for teachers.

In other words, teachers have a very difficult job, which is made more difficult because of the shifting policy terrain that dictates their official obligations. Imposing new strategies and practices for how we maintain security and punishment only adds to this burden. Since the recent school safety reforms do not come with the same pressures (i.e., threat of school funding and job performance appraisals) as academic reforms, it seems likely they will not be taken very seriously and may not result in much real change.

Ingrained School Culture

Another potential obstacle to meaningful school discipline and security reform is that much of it goes against the grain—it runs contrary to how things are done. Large bureaucracies can be very slow to change, particularly when their practices are so deeply ingrained that they are simply taken for granted. As I discuss in *Homeroom Security*, our contemporary school discipline practices are rooted in longstanding antagonisms between adults and children. Attitudes and behaviors supporting harsh punishment and rigid security are very deeply ingrained in what teachers do. New rules that tell adults or other school administrators to behave differently than they have learned to do over several years of training seem unlikely to accomplish much.

Resistance to Evidence

Another reason why I fear that recent reform may be limited is that these reforms contradict many taken-for-granted beliefs. Recall the email I shared at the start of chapter 2, in which a staff member at a national association preferred to rely on his individual experience rather than the available body of evidence. While I found this disappointing, given that he was responsible for assessing evidence on behalf of an important organization, this is a very common practice.

When I give presentations about my work and discuss some of the contents of this book, I am often met with skepticism. People often don't believe that schools are so much safer today than they were in the early 1990s, or that schools rely more on suspension and arrest today than they did a generation ago. These empirical facts run contrary to their taken-for-granted assumptions that kids today are out of control and that schools let children get away with murder. Many scholars have noted the persistence of "kids these days" myths, or nostalgic beliefs that youths today are less respectful, more disorderly, and less trustworthy than kids were when they were young.[6] Such nostalgia makes it more difficult to accept that most kids want to be in school and intend to behave there, or that treating them with respect and compassion is more effective at maintaining school safety than more punitive responses. Our use of failed security and discipline practices is based on these beliefs about out-of-control kids and on our reluctance to consider evidence of effective practices, making resistance to evidence a central problem to overcome.

Overcorrection

A final potential snag to school safety reform is the possibility that schools hear only half of the reform message—limiting punishments—and overcorrect in this direction. Yes, the push to reform is focused centrally on limiting punishments like suspension and expulsion that remove kids from school. But in no way does this mean (as I have reiterated throughout this book) that we should fail to respond to student misbehavior. We still need to consistently and firmly enforce school rules, but we need to do so more thoughtfully, rather than just kicking kids out of school. And when the offense is bad enough, we still need to suspend and occasionally expel students—but these cases need to be much less common than we see across the United States today. Maybe even more importantly, the reform agenda is not just about limiting punishments. It also seeks to replace some of the suspensions with problem solving. School disciplinary reform does not mean the end to school discipline. It means more effective intervention—adults in schools dealing with students constructively rather than kicking them out or ignoring them.

My concern is that schools will learn only half of this message and refrain from responding to student misbehavior in any real way. The evidence shows that restorative justice is effective. But it is difficult to do well. If reform means that schools replace punishment with a watered-down or ineffective version of punishment avoidance, students will fail to learn from their mistakes and will have too few boundaries on their behavior. In this case schools might become more—not less—chaotic and harmful for youths.[7] Progress may not be easy, but improving our schools and how we socialize our youths into citizens seems worth it.

CONCLUDING THOUGHTS

My goal throughout this book has been to fuel an open, evidence-based discussion about school safety. It is a topic that causes widespread anxiety, particularly after a horrific incident like the massacre at Newtown. And yet our efforts to maintain school safety are often misguided; much of what we do is harmful to children, families, and communities, while costing us a great deal of money. Until now, we had known a lot about the harms to individual students. In the preceding chapters, I summarized what we know and extended it by demonstrating harms to families, school communities, democratic society, and taxpayers.

While the evidence on many of the issues I have discussed—particularly the effectiveness of SROs—is not fully settled, we now know a great deal about how to better maintain school safety. What's more, school safety is a universally shared goal. Unlike other political arguments, on which liberals and conservatives hold opposite objectives or priorities, the topic of school safety would seem to be a politically easy topic. We all want to practice the most effective school security practices, while doing as little damage as possible to children, families, schools, and communities. With a more open dialogue, it may be possible to build on shared priorities to fix the real school safety problem and implement better practices.

Meaningful reform to school security and punishment is vitally important for many reasons. It could improve educational outcomes, help families, reduce bullying and other school misbehavior, improve democratic participation, and even save money. It is a crucial component of efforts to reduce racial inequality. As I have mentioned repeatedly, youths of color are considerably more likely than White youths to be punished in school, and as a result they and their families suffer more frequently than others all the harms described in this book: they are more likely to have the negative family effects described in chapter 4, to drop out of school or be exposed to the juvenile justice system, and to be discouraged from future civic participation. Unnecessary school punishment is an integral part of continuing racial inequality. Any efforts to address racial injustice— whether they are efforts to address perceptions of racially unjust policing, disparities in future incomes, or other problems—need to address school security and discipline.

Finally, it is important that we address these issues and fix the real school safety problem, not just for the good of the youths, families, and schools affected by it, but for all of us. As I have illustrated throughout this book, the overpolicing and punishment of youths harms society at large. It reduces democratic participation, siphons off talent from the labor market, and fuels a brand of inequality that is very damaging. Our efforts to build a better nation ought to include a serious commitment to more fair and effective school safety policies.

Appendix

In chapters 4, 5, and 6, my coauthors and I report on results of original data analysis. To allow for more readable, less dense chapters, I have saved a discussion of the research methods behind these analyses for this appendix. In the following sections, I discuss the data and analytical strategies that produced the results described in these three chapters.

CHAPTER 4: HURTING FAMILIES

In November 2012 and January 2013, I visited Mobile, Alabama. In January, I was accompanied by my graduate research assistant, Thomas J. Mowen, who is now an assistant professor at the University of Wyoming. We were invited by the Southern Poverty Law Center (SPLC) to speak to parents of children punished at school. These parents were working with the SPLC on a lawsuit against the Mobile schools, and many were also participating in community programs that taught parents their rights regarding their (and their children's) treatment in schools.

We began recruitment in 2012 after approval from the University of Delaware's Human Subjects Research Board. I wrote a recruitment letter that explained our research and requested voluntary participation. The

SPLC distributed this letter to participants of the lawsuit and mentioned it in community meetings. The letter included my cell phone number and asked parents to call me to schedule an appointment if they were willing to discuss their experiences. Several parents called, and I scheduled interviews to take place during one of the two trips to Mobile.

While in Mobile, we conducted most of the interviews with parents in their homes. Some were instead conducted at a parent's place of work or in a restaurant. Before the interviews, all parents read and signed informed consent forms that spelled out their rights as research subjects, including the anonymity we would provide (all names used in the chapters are pseudonyms), and confirmed that the interview was voluntary. Some parents asked their children to participate as well, and one included other family members. All participants signed an informed consent form; parents and children both filled out forms (an assent form for minors, a parental consent form for parents) before children could be interviewed. All interviews were recorded and later transcribed into text documents by us.

We then analyzed the transcribed data using Atlas.ti qualitative analysis software. This software allows researchers to scan transcripts and code data by highlighting and categorizing meaningful segments that can later be compared and contrasted across interviews. This process, refined through repetition and analysis by both of us, allowed us to produce the pattern of findings that we report in chapter 4.

As we mention in chapter 4, these interviews serve a specific purpose: to highlight the experiences of parents whose children have been punished in school. These parents do not represent a random sample of the population—they were all motivated to speak to us and were participating in a lawsuit against the schools. As a nonrandom sample, they do not represent parents' views generally. Yet these interviews are extremely useful, because they paint a picture of how some families can be hurt by excessive school punishment. The extent to which this is generalizable to other populations and places is something that future studies should consider.

CHAPTER 5: HOW SCHOOLS TEACH BULLYING

In chapter 5, Katie A. Farina and I describe analyses that we conducted on school punishment, security, and bullying victimization, which were published in a recent issue of the journal *Youth Violence and Juvenile Justice*.[1] We analyzed data collected in 2009 by the U.S. Census Bureau and Bureau of Justice Statistics: the School Crime Supplement (SCS) to the National Crime Victimization Survey (NCVS). While the NCVS is an annual survey, and one of the most extensive sources of data available on criminal victimization, the SCS is conducted only every two years. After completion of the NCVS within a sampled household, the SCS questions are then posed to members of the sampled households who are twelve to eighteen years old and enrolled in a primary or secondary school within six months prior to the interview. Its main focus is criminal victimization of young people while at school.

There were a total of 8,986 youths eligible to respond to the SCS; 55.9 percent of them (5,023) completed the interview. Beginning with these cases, we removed cases of respondents who were homeschooled, who were in postsecondary education, or who failed to respond to relevant questions. Our final sample for analysis included $N = 4,284$ cases.

The SCS includes several questions about bullying. The first series of these questions begins with the statement "Now I have some questions about what students do at school that make you feel bad or are hurtful to you. We often refer to this as being bullied. You may include events you told me about already. During this school year, has any student bullied you? That is, has another student. . . ." The survey then asks about specific forms of bullying, including whether someone has "made fun of you"; "spread rumors about you"; "threatened you with harm"; "pushed you, shoved you, tripped you, or spit on you"; "tried to make you do things you did not want to do"; "excluded you from activities on purpose"; and "destroyed your property on purpose." In a separate series of questions, respondents are asked about hurtful events that "could occur anywhere." The specific actions include "posted hurtful information . . . on a social networking site"; "threatened or insulted you through e-mail"; "threatened or insulted you through instant messaging"; "threatened or insulted you through text messaging"; "threatened or insulted you through online gaming . . ."; and "purposefully excluded you from an online community." Each of these questions is answered yes/no.

We took these questions and created four dependent variables. The first indicates whether the respondent reported any form of in-person bullying (any of the first series of questions); the second indicates reports of any in-person *physical* bullying (including threats of harm, pushing/shoving/tripping/spitting on, being forced to do things against one's will, and destruction of property); the third indicates reports of any in-person *verbal* bullying (being made fun of, spreading of rumors, and intentional exclusion from activities); and the fourth indicates report of any cyberbullying (any of the second series of questions). Tests of internal consistency found reasonable to high reliability scores for each of these measures (Cronbach's alpha scores were 0.75, 0.61, 0.65, and 0.98, respectively).

Our primary independent variables measure students' perceptions of school rules and punishments. Respondents were asked the following series of questions, each of which is answered along a four-point scale of agreement (from strongly disagree to strongly agree): "everyone knows what the school rules are"; "the rules are fair"; "the punishment for breaking rules is the same no matter who you are"; "the rules are strictly enforced"; and "if a rule is broken, students know what punishment will follow." We also included a variable measuring how many of the following security practices were used at the respondents' schools: police officers or security guards, metal detectors, locked entrances or exits during the day, locker checks, a requirement that students wear ID badges, and security cameras. Finally, we created a series of variables to capture the relationship between two indicators from the survey, one that measured student classroom disruption frequency and another that measured teacher punishment frequency. This new series of three variables includes (1) lenient teachers (students report frequent disruptions but infrequent punishment), (2) balance (students' reports of disruptions and punishment match), and (3) punitive teachers (students report infrequent disruptions but frequent punishment).

Our analyses also included many independent variables to best control for individual and school factors that might shape bullying victimization and better isolate the relationship between perceptions of school rules and bullying victimization. These variables include students' reported bonds to teachers, respondents' demographics (age, grade level, race, and ethnicity), grade point average, extent of extracurricular activity participation, and public or private school. Finally, we included several variables to account for student misbehavior and school dangerousness: whether gangs are known to be present in the school, whether drugs or alcohol are available there, whether the respondent knows of any guns being brought to school, and whether the respondent had been in a fight in the past year.

After performing all relevant diagnostic tests and using the provided sample weight variables, we then computed a series of logistic regression models. All analyses were done using Stata SE 13.1. In chapter 5, we describe the relevant results and illustrate the predicted probability of youths reporting bullying victimization, given their perception of school rules. Table A.1 lists the full regression model results used to derive these results.

There are a few important limitations of these analyses that need to be noted. One is that we are analyzing data on victimization, not bullying behaviors. A second is that we are considering students' perceptions of school rules and punishments rather than schools' actions. A third is that our data were collected at one point in time and thus are less able to confirm causal relationships than data collected over time. Despite these limitations, there are important reasons why we are confident in our results. One is that they are robust and consistent. A second is that they mirror exactly what we expected to find, based on the existing literature and the most similar previous analyses on unfair punishments and school disorder.

CHAPTER 6: CIVIC PARTICIPATION IN THE FUTURE

For the analyses reported in chapter 6, a different version of which were recently published in the journal *Youth & Society*,[2] we used data from the National Longitudinal Survey of Adolescent to Adult Health (Add Health). Add Health is a nationally representative, longitudinal survey conducted by the University of North Carolina Population Center and funded by several federal agencies. In 1994–95, students in grades 7–12 were sampled for inclusion in the study. A total of 90,118 students from eighty randomly selected schools were included, with 20,745 randomly selected for in-home interviews at multiple times. These students were reinterviewed three additional times, in 1996 (wave 2), 2001–02 (wave 3), and 2007–08 (wave 4). Their parents and school administrators were interviewed as well. Because it is well designed, rigorously executed, and broad in scope, this dataset has been used frequently by scholars in a wide variety of disciplines to address many different research issues.[3]

Table A.1 Logistic Regression of Reported Bullying Victimization

	Any in-person bullying	Any in-person verbal bullying	Any in-person physical bullying	Any cyberbullying
Race (contrast = White)				
Black	0.872	0.862	0.941	0.613 *
Other race	0.646 **	0.640 **	0.706	0.694
Hispanic	0.754 **	0.758 *	0.800	0.637 *
Female	1.228 **	1.315 ***	0.940	1.805 ***
Age	0.848 ***	0.865 ***	0.790 ***	0.938
Lower grade level	1.592 ***	1.604 ***	1.535 **	1.245
Region (contrast = Urban)				
Suburban	1.152	1.151	1.142	1.364
Rural	1.266	1.322 *	1.125	0.994
Public school	1.219	1.180	1.108	0.918
Grade point average	0.766 ***	0.759 ***	0.777 ***	0.755 **
Number of extracurriculars	1.308 ***	1.291 ***	1.321 ***	1.378 ***
Gangs	1.610 ***	1.605 ***	1.771 ***	1.664 **
Drugs available	2.820 ***	2.583 ***	2.785 ***	3.760 ***
Fighting	7.653 ***	4.580 ***	9.374 ***	2.780 ***
Gun to school	1.307	1.283	1.405	1.906 **
Punishment fairness:				
Everyone knows school rules	0.962	0.965	0.937	1.154
School rules are fair	0.776 **	0.822 *	0.845	0.750 *
Punishment same for all	0.973	0.915	0.941	0.891
School rules strictly enforced	0.942	0.930	0.925	1.101
Known punishment	0.781 **	0.801 **	0.718 ***	0.782 *
Teacher punishment (contrast = Balanced)				
Too lenient	1.363 **	1.426 **	1.162	1.269
Too punitive	1.000	1.008	0.868	0.883
Number of security practices	0.974	0.967	0.995	1.013
Bonds to teachers	1.069	1.054	0.884	0.877
Constant	18.692 ***	13.658 ***	45.362 ***	0.450
Log-likelihood	−2,159.180	−2,110.292	−1,408.236	−835.883
N	4,255	4,255	4,255	4,255

NOTE: Values are odds ratios (Exp(B)). *$P < .05$, **$P < .01$, ***$P < .001$.

We used all cases of adolescents that had complete data and were interviewed through the final wave of data collection. Our sample sizes are N = 9,006 for wave 3 (2001–02) outcomes and N = 7,361 for wave 4 (2007–08) outcomes.

In our analyses we used dependent variables from wave 3 (2001–02), when the respondents were eighteen to twenty-six years old; and from wave 4 (2007–08), when they were twenty-four to thirty-three years old. The wave 3 variables are dichotomous indicators (identifying only "yes" or "no") of whether the respondents registered to vote, voted in the most recent presidential election, and performed any volunteer or community service work in the past twelve months. The wave 4 variables include one measured along a four-point scale (from 1 = never to 4 = always) that asks how often the respondent votes in local or statewide elections, and one measured along a six-point scale (1 = 0 hours to 6 = 160 hours or more) that asks how many hours respondents spent on volunteer or community service work in the past twelve months.

Our primary independent variable is whether respondents had been suspended from school by wave 1. We included several variables measuring schools' security and punishment practices from the wave 1 school administrator survey: whether it is a closed campus, presence of a dress code, and whether a student who is caught on a first offense of cheating/fighting/verbally abusing a teacher/smoking is suspended or expelled (with punishment for each offense included as a separate variable). From the wave 2 school administrator survey, we included measures of whether the school has a security officer or school resource officer, metal detectors, surveillance cameras, or anti-gang rules.

We also included dozens of variables that allowed us to control for variation among students and schools, and therefore factor out other competing explanations for variations in future civic participation. These include race/ethnicity, age, and sex; primary language spoken; parents' education level; grade point average; whether the respondent lives with his or her mother or father; students' plans to attend college; area (urban/rural/suburban); the school's average attendance rate; the school's average class size; public vs. private school; frequency of the respondent's religious service attendance; parents' level of civic participation; participation in extracurricular activities; students' views of their school as a community;

students' views of whether teachers treat them fairly; respondents' autonomy from their parents; the range of topics they discuss with their parents; self-esteem; neighborhood bonds; marijuana use; cocaine use; inhalant use; other drug use; a general delinquency index that measures the extent of their offending history; and prior incarceration.

Because our data are nested—they consist of reports of students within schools—we performed multilevel models, using Stata 12.1. For the dichotomous wave 3 outcomes we used random intercept logistic models, and for the ordinal wave 4 variables we used random intercept ordinal logistic regression models (using Stata's gllamm command with an ologit link). All models use the provided wave-specific sampling weights. We ran each model on its own, and then with interaction terms of Black respondent × suspension and Hispanic respondent × suspension; these are labeled "full model" in table A.2, which shows the wave 3 results, and in table A.3, which shows the wave 4 results.

Having found that suspension predicts decreased future civic participation at both wave 3 and wave 4, we continued to explore our data to test whether this result might be due to respondents' deviance rather than to suspension. That is, if only students who misbehave more than others get suspended, perhaps it is something about these kids that exists prior to suspension that is related to future civic participation, rather than an effect of suspension itself. To consider this, we used propensity-score matching analysis. This process predicts the likelihood of suspension based on the available data and forms two matched groups—those who were in fact suspended and those who were not suspended—with similar propensities for suspensions. That is, members of the two groups are matched in pairs, where members of the pairs are very similar on all relevant characteristics except whether they were actually suspended. The analysis then compares these two groups regarding the dependent variables. The results mirror results from our regression models.

We also considered whether suspension mediates between deviance and future civic participation by using structural equation modeling. Here we included suspension as an intervening variable, existing between deviance (delinquency and each drug-use variable) and civic participation. Again the results confirm our original findings.

Table A.2 Random-Intercept Logistic Regression of Wave 3 Civic Participation on School Punishment and Security Indicators and Control Variables

	Voted		*Registered to vote*		*Volunteered*	
		FULL MODEL		FULL MODEL		FULL MODEL
Ever suspended	-0.127 *	-0.051	-0.090	-0.058	-0.194 *	-0.203
Verbal punishment	-0.100	-0.098	-0.098	-0.096	-0.089	-0.088
Cheating punishment	-0.416 *	-0.416 *	-0.227	-0.227	-0.286	-0.285
Fighting punishment	0.024	0.024	0.081	0.081	0.095	0.094
Smoking punishment	0.071	0.066	0.020	0.014	0.171 *	0.170 *
Dress code	-0.059	-0.059	-0.168	-0.169	-0.128	-0.129
Closed campus	0.244	0.244	0.032	0.034	0.222	0.225
Officer	-0.030	-0.032	-0.071	-0.074	0.053	0.053
Metal detectors	0.121	0.124	0.100	0.104	-0.132	-0.130
Surveillance	0.095	0.095	0.100	0.099	-0.120	-0.121
Anti-gang rules	0.009	0.005	0.026	0.022	-0.078	-0.079
Black × suspended		-0.193		-0.216		-0.070
Hispanic × suspended		-0.048		0.185		0.221
Age	0.134 ***	0.134 ***	0.089 ***	0.089 ***	-0.028	-0.028
Sex	0.054	0.056	0.088	0.090	0.028	0.029
Foreign language	-0.527 ***	-0.525 ***	-0.561 ***	-0.556 ***	0.056	0.059
Hispanic	0.118	0.123	0.067	0.009	-0.046	-0.094
Black	0.283 ***	0.340 ***	0.192 **	0.274 **	0.003	0.027
American Indian	0.207	0.202	0.276	0.279	0.252	0.255

(continued)

Table A.2   (continued)

	Voted		Registered to vote		Volunteered	
	FULL MODEL	FULL MODEL	FULL MODEL	FULL MODEL	FULL MODEL	FULL MODEL
Asian American	−0.529 ***	−0.528 ***	−0.314 **	−0.314 **	0.011	0.010
Other race/ethnicity	−0.296 *	−0.300 *	−0.395 **	−0.401 **	−0.267	−0.268
Does not live with mother	−0.131	−0.134	−0.102	−0.107	−0.049	−0.050
Does not live with father	−0.047	−0.047	−0.062	−0.064	−0.008	−0.009
Parent educational level	0.143 ***	0.143 ***	0.092 ***	0.092 ***	0.182 ***	0.182 ***
Grades	−0.196 ***	−0.198 ***	−0.136 ***	−0.137 ***	−0.427 ***	−0.427 ***
School community	0.024	0.022	−0.004	−0.005	0.012	0.012
Teacher fairness	0.017	0.017	−0.024	−0.024	−0.026	−0.026
Marijuana use (ln)	0.034	0.032	0.043	0.042	−0.060	−0.060
Cocaine use (ln)	−0.037	−0.042	0.007	−0.002	−0.425	−0.428
Inhalant use (ln)	0.027	0.026	0.022	0.020	0.025	0.024
Other drug use (ln)	−0.051	−0.055	−0.004	−0.007	0.002	−0.001
Delinquency scale	−0.097	−0.095	0.010	0.009	−0.024	−0.023
Wants college	0.095 **	0.097 **	0.089 ***	0.091 ***	0.066	0.067
Autonomy from parents	−0.006	−0.007	−0.006	−0.006	−0.010	−0.010
Discussions with parents	0.033 *	0.033 *	0.018	0.019	0.027	0.028
Low self-esteem	−0.044	−0.043	−0.062	−0.062	−0.146 **	−0.146 **
Neighborhood bonds	0.055 **	0.056 **	0.048 **	0.048 **	0.035	0.035
Parents' civic participation	0.089 **	0.090 **	0.114 ***	0.113 ***	0.111 ***	0.110 ***
Honor society	0.198 *	0.197 *	0.302 **	0.301 **	0.196 *	0.196 *

Student council	0.012	0.011	0.130	0.126	0.093	0.091
Future Farmers	0.012	0.014	-0.137	-0.134	-0.077	-0.077
Performing arts	0.179 **	0.181	0.151 **	0.153 **	0.323 ***	0.323 ***
News/yearbook	-0.004	-0.003	-0.037	-0.038	0.075	0.074
Academic clubs	0.073	0.073	0.046	0.048	-0.115	-0.113
Sports teams	-0.031	-0.030	-0.011	-0.011	0.188 **	0.187 **
Other clubs	0.163 **	0.165 **	0.125	0.125	0.234 ***	0.234 **
Religious service attendance	0.109 ***	0.108 ***	0.094 ***	0.093 ***	0.087 ***	0.087 ***
Public school	-0.299 **	-0.298 **	-0.107	-0.102	-0.102	-0.101
Suburban	0.104	0.106	0.105	0.107	-0.068	-0.067
Rural	0.168	0.172	0.301 *	0.304 *	-0.003	-0.001
Average attendance rate	-0.073	-0.070	-0.059	-0.054	-0.094	-0.092
Average class size	0.016 *	0.016 *	0.005	0.005	-0.002	-0.002
Prior incarceration	-0.723	-0.705	-0.223	-0.211	0.714	0.714
Constant	-3.934 ***	-3.953 ***	-1.874 ***	-1.899 ***	-0.777	-0.785
Random intercept (SD)	0.206	0.206	0.236	0.235	0.149	0.147
Log-likelihood	-5,513.252	-5,512.109	-5,812.217	-5,808.935	-4,542.469	-4,541.556

NOTE: Values are log odds. *$P < .05$, **$P < .01$, ***$P < .001$; $N = 9{,}006$.

Table A.3 Random-Intercept Ordinal Logistic Regression of Wave 4 Civic Participation on School Punishment and Security Indicators and Control Variables

	Voting frequency		Volunteer frequency	
	FULL MODEL		FULL MODEL	
Ever suspended	−0.111	−0.206 *	0.056	−0.037
Verbal punishment	−0.111	−0.109	−0.180 *	−0.180 *
Cheating punishment	0.136	0.135	0.151	0.148
Fighting punishment	0.060	0.061	−0.059	−0.058
Smoking punishment	0.128	0.130	−0.002	0.002
Dress code	−0.118	−0.122	0.057	0.054
Closed campus	0.178	0.187	−0.119	−0.114
Officer	−0.172	−0.171	0.165	0.167
Metal detectors	0.343 **	0.342 **	0.000	−0.002
Surveillance	0.276 *	0.272 *	0.103	0.103
Anti-gang rules	−0.270 *	−0.267 *	−0.050	−0.045
Black × suspended		0.092		0.149
Hispanic × suspended		0.397 **		0.298
Age	0.088 ***	0.089 ***	0.018	0.018
Sex	0.128 **	0.128 **	0.080	0.078
Foreign language	−0.341 **	−0.339 **	−0.292 *	−0.294 *
Hispanic	0.019	−0.077	−0.319 **	−0.383 ***
Black	0.514 ***	0.499 ***	−0.179 *	−0.213 *
American Indian	0.171	0.181	0.001	0.009
Asian American	−0.695 ***	−0.699 ***	−0.177	−0.178
Other race/ethnicity	−0.181	−0.180	0.139	0.141
Does not live with mother	−0.044	−0.047	0.133	0.134
Does not live with father	0.009	0.007	−0.026	−0.026
Parent educational level	0.169 ***	0.169 ***	0.097 ***	0.097 ***
Grades	−0.145 ***	−0.143 ***	−0.283 ***	−0.281 ***
School community	0.024	0.024	−0.046	−0.045
Teacher fairness	−0.012	−0.012	−0.011	−0.010
Marijuana use (ln)	0.008	0.009	−0.005	−0.004
Cocaine use (ln)	0.021	0.012	−0.165	−0.164
Inhalant use (ln)	−0.006	−0.006	0.009	0.010
Other drug use (ln)	0.072	0.074	0.052	0.053
Delinquency scale	−0.019	−0.025	0.047	0.044
Wants college	0.164 ***	0.163 ***	0.067 *	0.065 *
Autonomy from parents	0.015	0.015	0.005	0.005
Discussions with parents	0.033 *	0.034 *	0.076 ***	0.077 ***

Low self-esteem	−0.083	−0.083	−0.029	−0.030
Neighborhood bonds	0.030	0.030	0.041 *	0.041 *
Parents' civic participation	0.099 ***	0.097 ***	0.101 ***	0.099 ***
Honor society	0.168 *	0.168 *	0.265 **	0.266 **
Student council	−0.006	−0.009	0.236 **	0.235 **
Future Farmers	0.096	0.094	0.078	0.075
Performing arts	0.180 **	0.179 **	0.192 **	0.191 **
News/yearbook	0.113	0.112	−0.026	−0.027
Academic clubs	0.041	0.041	0.060	0.061
Sports teams	0.018	0.017	0.076	0.076
Other clubs	0.145 *	0.141 *	0.296 ***	0.293 ***
Religious service attendance	0.118 ***	0.118 ***	0.130 ***	0.130 ***
Public school	−0.248 *	−0.249 *	−0.035	−0.035
Suburban	0.007	0.005	−0.035	−0.036
Rural	0.132	0.130	−0.128	−0.130
Average attendance rate	0.010	0.011	−0.071	−0.071
Average class size	0.012	0.011	−0.003	−0.004
Prior incarceration	−1.301 ***	−1.302 ***	−0.595 *	−0.597 *
Constant 1	2.048 ***	2.031 ***	1.244 **	1.230
Constant 2	3.277 ***	3.260 ***	2.671 ***	2.657
Constant 3	4.138 ***	4.122 ***	3.276 ***	3.262
Constant 4			3.934 ***	3.920
Constant 5			4.605 ***	4.591
Random intercept (var)	0.069	0.068	0.046	0.046
Log-likelihood	−9,526.410	−9,523.061	−7,670.389	−7,668.941

NOTE: Values are log odds. *$P < .05$, **$P < .01$, ***$P < .001$; $N = 7,361$.

Notes

CHAPTER 1. INTRODUCTION

1. Reported on CBS New York, December 22, 2012. Accessed online at http://newyork.cbslocal.com/2012/12/22/quinn-nra-plan-to-avoid-mass-shootings-is-stupid-asinine/.

2. Peter Rugg and James Nye (2012) "'The most revolting, tone deaf statement I've ever seen': NRA condemned after astonishing response to Sandy Hook massacre calling for schools to arm themselves." *Daily Mail Online*, December 21. Accessed online at www.dailymail.co.uk/news/article-2251762/NRA-condemned-astonishing-response-Sandy-Hook-massacre-calling-schools-arm-themselves.html.

3. B. H. et al. v. City of New York et al., 10–0210. Accessed online at www.nyclu.org/files/Amended_Complaint.pdf.

4. See Elora Mukherjee (2007) "Criminalizing the classroom: The over-policing of New York City schools." New York, NY: New York Civil Liberties Union; Kathleen Nolan (2011) *Police in the Hallways: Discipline in an Urban High School*. Minneapolis, MN: University of Minnesota Press.

5. Stated in an interview on *Nightline*, December 21, 2012. Accessed online at http://abcnews.go.com/Nightline/video/nyc-mayor-michael-bloomberg-nra-18041670.

6. See Aaron Kupchik (2010) *Homeroom Security: School Discipline in an Age of Fear*. New York, NY: NYU Press.

7. Gallup (August 29, 2013) "Parents' school safety fears haven't receded since Newtown: One in three K–12 parents fear for child's safety at school." Accessed online at www.gallup.com/poll/164168/parents-school-safety-fears-havent-receded-newtown.aspx. See also Lynn A. Addington (2009) "Cops and cameras: Public school security as a policy response to Columbine." *American Behavioral Scientist* 52: 1426–1446.

8. See David Altheide (2002) *Creating Fear: News and the Construction of Crisis*. New York, NY: Aldine de Gruyter.

9. See Kupchik (2010).

10. See www.splcenter.org/sites/default/files/downloads/case/mace_thirda-mended110729.PDF; on September 30, 2015, U.S. District Judge Abdul K. Kallon released his decision in support of the plaintiffs, agreeing with the students and the Southern Poverty Law Center that the use of pepper spray was excessive.

11. Prior studies have uncovered deeply held stereotypes about the dangerousness of Black youth, particularly low-income Black youth, among police officers and others. See Joshua Correll, Bernadette Park, Charles M. Judd, Bernd Wittenbrink, Melody S. Sadler, and Tracie Keesee (2007) "Across the thin blue line: Police officers and racial bias in the decision to shoot." *Journal of Personality and Social Psychology* 92: 1006–1023; for a review of stereotypes and law enforcement, see Michelle Alexander (2010) *The New Jim Crow: Mass Incarceration in the Age of Colorblindness*. New York, NY: New Press.

12. See Polly Mosendz (2015) "Report: South Carolina student flipped by police officer is in foster care." *Newsweek*, October 28. Accessed online at www.newsweek.com/south-carolina-student-flipped-police-officer-foster-care-388119.

13. See table 2.1 in Simone Robers, Anlan Zhang, Rachel Morgan, and Lauren Musu-Gillette (2015) "Indicators of school crime and safety: 2014." Washington, DC: National Center for Education Statistics, U.S. Department of Education.

14. See Robers et al. (2015): figures 13.1 and 14.1.

15. See Robers et al. (2015): figure 1.1.

16. Sherry L. Murphy, Jiaquan Xu, and Kenneth D. Kochanek (2013) "Deaths: Final data for 2010." *National Vital Statistics Reports* 61(4). U.S. Centers for Disease Control and Prevention: Division of Vital Statistics. Accessed online at www.cdc.gov/nchs/data/nvsr/nvsr61/nvsr61_04.pdf.

17. On teenage pregnancy, see www.cdc.gov/teenpregnancy/; on sexual activity, see www.cdc.gov/nchs/nsfg/key_statistics/t.htm#teenagers; on drug and alcohol use, see www.cdc.gov/HealthyYouth/alcoholdrug/index.htm.

18. See Daniel J. Losen and Tia Elena Martinez (2013) "Out of school & off-track: The overuse of suspensions in American middle and high schools." Los Angeles, CA: UCLA Center for Civil Rights Remedies at the Civil Rights Project.

19. Robers et al. (2015): table 20.3.

20. See New York City School-Justice Partnership Task Force (2013) "Keeping kids in school and out of court." Albany, NY: New York State Permanent Judicial Commission on Justice for Children.

21. See Kupchik (2010); Nolan (2011).

22. Richard Arum (2003) *Judging School Discipline: The Crisis of Moral Authority*. Cambridge, MA: Harvard University Press.

23. For further discussion and analysis of the spread of policies across schools, and distinctions among them, see Katherine Irwin, Janet Davidson, and Amanda Hall-Sanchez (2013) "The race to punish in American schools: Class and race predictors of punitive school-crime control." *Critical Criminology* 21: 47–71; Aaron Kupchik (2009) "Things are tough all over: Race, ethnicity, class, and school discipline." *Punishment & Society* 11: 291–317; Aaron Kupchik and Geoff Ward (2014) "Race, poverty, and exclusionary school security: An empirical analysis of U.S. elementary, middle, and high schools." *Youth Violence and Juvenile Justice* 12: 332–354; Allison A. Payne and Kelly Welch (2010) "Modeling the effects of racial threat on punitive and restorative school discipline practices." *Criminology* 48: 1019–1062; Kelly Welch and Allison A. Payne (2010) "Racial threat and punitive school discipline." *Social Problems* 57: 25–48; Kelly Welch and Allison A. Payne (2012) "Exclusionary school punishment: The effect of racial threat on expulsion and suspension." *Youth Violence and Juvenile Justice* 10: 155–171.

24. See Jonathan Simon (2007) *Governing through Crime: How the War on Crime Transformed American Democracy and Created a Culture of Fear*. New York, NY: Oxford University Press; the author gives a brilliant analysis of how fear and anxiety are used to justify greater punishment, including an explosion of prison populations and school punishment.

25. See David Harvey (2005) *A Brief History of Neoliberalism*. Oxford: Oxford University Press.

26. See David Garland (2001) *The Culture of Control: Crime and Social Order in Contemporary Society*. Chicago, IL: University of Chicago Press.

CHAPTER 2. EFFECTIVE SCHOOL CRIME PREVENTION

1. Note that some details about the individual are altered to protect his identity, but the email exchange is reported verbatim.

2. See Arum (2003); Gerald Grant (1990) *The World We Created at Hamilton High*. Cambridge, MA: Harvard University Press; Kupchik (2010).

3. Philip Babcock (2009) "The rational adolescent: Discipline policies, lawsuits, and skill acquisition." *Economics of Education Review* 28: 551–560. See also Arum (2003); Gregory M. Zimmerman and Carter Rees (2014) "Do school disciplinary policies have positive social impacts? Examining the attenuating

effects of school policies on the relationship between personal and peer delinquency." *Journal of Criminal Justice* 42: 54–65.

4. Further, both recent findings supporting strict rules—Babcock (2009) and Zimmerman and Rees (2014)—use the same dataset, the National Longitudinal Survey of Adolescent Health. It's not clear whether the same result might be found in other datasets.

5. Philip J. Cook, Denise C. Gottfredson, and Chongmin Na (2010) "School crime control and prevention." *Crime and Justice* 39: 313–440 (see p. 369).

6. He was also given a lifetime NRA membership: www.nydailynews.com /news/national/ boy-suspended-gun-shaped-pop-tart-lifetime-nra-membership-article-1.1359918.

7. See American Psychological Association Zero Tolerance Task Force (2008) "Are zero tolerance policies effective in the schools? An evidentiary review and recommendations." *American Psychologist* 63: 852–862.

8. For example, Michael Rocque and Raymond Paternoster (2011) "Understanding the antecedents of the 'school-to-jail' link: The relationship between race and school discipline." *Journal of Criminal Law and Criminology* 101: 633–665.

9. For example, Sandra M. Way (2011) "School discipline and disruptive classroom behavior: The moderating effects of student perceptions." *The Sociological Quarterly* 52: 346–375.

10. For example, Christine Bowditch (1993) "Getting rid of troublemakers: High school disciplinary procedures and the production of dropouts." *Social Problems* 40: 493–509; Edward W. Morris (2005) "'Tuck in that shirt!' Race, class, gender, and discipline in an urban school." *Sociological Perspectives* 48: 25–48; Russell J. Skiba, Robert S. Michael, Abra Carroll Nardo, and Reece Peterson (2000) "The color of discipline: Sources of racial and gender disproportionality in school punishment." Research Report SRS1. Bloomington, IN: Indiana Education Policy Center.

11. For example, Tony Fabelo, Michael D. Thompson, Martha Plotkin, Dottie Carmichael, Miner P. Marchbanks III, and Eric A. Booth (2011) "Breaking schools' rules: A statewide study of how school discipline relates to students' success and juvenile justice involvement." New York, NY: Council of State Governments Justice Center and Public Policy Research; Rocque and Paternoster (2011).

12. For example, Bowditch (1993); Ann Arnett Ferguson (2000) *Bad Boys: Public Schools in the Making of Black Masculinity.* Ann Arbor, MI: University of Michigan Press; Amanda E. Lewis (2003) *Race in the Schoolyard: Negotiating the Color Line in Classrooms and Communities.* New Brunswick, NJ: Rutgers University Press; John D. McCarthy and Dean R. Hoge (1987) "The social construct of school punishment: Racial disadvantage out of universalistic process." *Social Forces* 65: 1101–1120; Skiba et al. (2000).

13. For reviews, see Aaron Kupchik (2014) "The school-to-prison pipeline: Rhetoric and reality." In Franlin E. Zimring and David S. Tanenhaus (eds.), *Choosing the Future for American Juvenile Justice.* New York, NY: NYU Press; Catherin Y. Kim, Daniel J. Losen, and Damon T. Hewitt (2010) *The School-to-Prison Pipeline: Structuring Legal Reform.* New York, NY: NYU Press.

14. Kupchik (2010); Linda M. Raffaele Mendez and Howard M. Knoff (2003) "Who gets suspended from school and why: A demographic analysis of schools and disciplinary infractions in a large school district." *Education and Treatment of Children* 26: 30–51.

15. See New York City School-Justice Partnership Task Force (2013). The Council for State Governments has likewise addressed this issue with thorough, nonpartisan work; see Emily Morgan, Nina Solomon, Martha Plotkin, and Rebecca Cohen (2014) "The School Discipline Consensus Report: Strategies from the field to keep students engaged in school and out of the juvenile justice system." New York, NY: Council of State Governments Justice Center.

16. For a thorough review, see Cook et al. (2010).

17. Sheryl A. Hemphill, John W. Toumbourou, Todd I. Herrenkohl, Barbara J. McMorris, and Richard J. Catalano (2006) "The effect of school suspensions and arrests on subsequent adolescent antisocial behavior in Australia and the United States." *Journal of Adolescent Health* 39: 736–744.

18. Greg Chen (2008) "Communities, students, schools, and school crime: A confirmatory study of crime in U.S. high schools." *Urban Education* 43: 301–318.

19. Gary D. Gottfredson, Denise C. Gottfredson, Allison Ann Payne, and Nisha C. Gottfredson (2005) "School climate predictors of school disorder: Results from a national study of delinquency prevention in schools." *Journal of Research in Crime and Delinquency* 42: 412–444; Katie James, Jackson Bunch, and Jody Clay-Warner (2015) "Perceived injustice and school violence: An application of general strain theory." *Youth Violence and Juvenile Justice* 13: 169–189; Way (2011); Wayne N. Welsh (2001) "Effects of student and school factors on five measures of school disorder." *Justice Quarterly* 18: 911–947.

20. See Michelle Fine, April Burns, Yasser A. Payne, and Maria E. Torre (2004) "Civics lessons: The color and class of betrayal." *Teachers College Record* 106: 2193–2223; Nolan (2011); Victor M. Rios (2011) *Punished: Policing the Lives of Black and Latino Boys.* New York, NY: NYU Press; Carla Shedd (2015) *Unequal City: Race, Schools, and Perceptions of Injustice.* New York, NY: Russell Sage Foundation.

21. Kupchik (2010).

22. Kupchik (2010).

23. Kupchik (2010).

24. See Nolan (2011).

25. Ronet Bachman, Antonia Randolph, and Bethany L. Brown (2011) "Predicting perceptions of fear at school and going to and from school for African

American and White students: The effects of school security measures." *Youth & Society* 43: 705–726.

26. Nathan James and Gail McCallion (2013) "School resource officers: Law enforcement officers in schools." Washington DC: Congressional Research Service. See also Cook et al. (2010); Anthony Petrosino, Sarah Guckenburg, and Trevor Fronius (2012) "'Policing schools' strategies: A review of the evaluation evidence." *Journal of MultiDisciplinary Evaluation* 8: 80–101.

27. For example, John G. Schuiteman (2001) "Second annual evaluation of DCJS funded school resource officer programs." Report of the Department of Criminal Justice Services, fiscal year 1999–2000. Richmond, VA: Virginia State Department of Criminal Justice Services.

28. Ida M. Johnson (1999) "School violence: The effectiveness of a school resource officer program in a southern city." *Journal of Criminal Justice* 27: 173–192.

29. Marie Skubak Tillyer, Bonnie S. Fisher, and Pamela Wilcox (2011) "The effects of school crime prevention on students' violent victimization, risk perception and fear of crime: A multilevel opportunity perspective." *Justice Quarterly* 28: 249–277.

30. Wesley G. Jennings, David N. Khey, Jon Maskaly, and Christopher M. Donner (2011) "Evaluating the relationship between law enforcement and school security measures and violent crime in schools." *Journal of Police Crisis Negotiations* 11: 109–124.

31. Chongmin Na and Denise C. Gottfredson (2013) "Police officers in schools: Effects on school crime and the processing of offending behaviors." *Justice Quarterly* 30: 619–650.

32. See also Kevin P. Brady, Sharon Balmer, and Deinya Phenix (2007) "School–police partnership effectiveness in urban schools: An analysis of New York City's Impact Schools initiative." *Education and Urban Society* 39: 455–478. Brady et al. find that after the introduction of greater police presence in New York City "impact schools," these schools witnessed decreases in SAT scores and attendance, but increases in suspensions; they find no change in recorded crime after the introduction of more police officers.

33. Nolan (2011).

34. Rios (2011).

35. Mark H. Moore, Carol V. Petrie, Anthony A. Braga, and Brenda L. McLaughlin (2003) *Deadly Lessons: Understanding Lethal School Violence.* Washington, DC: National Academies Press; Kathleen Newman, Cybelle Fox, David Harding, Jal Mehta, and Wendy Roth (2004) *Rampage: The Social Roots of School Shootings.* New York, NY: Basic Books.

36. Newman et al. (2004).

37. Eric Madfis (2014) "Averting school rampage: Student intervention amid a persistent code of silence." *Youth Violence and Juvenile Justice* 12: 229–249.

38. For example, Amanda Petteruti (2011) "Education under arrest: The case against police in schools." Washington, DC: Justice Policy Institute.

39. For example, Maurice Canady, Bernard James, and Janet Nease (2012) "To protect & educate: The school resource officer and the prevention of violence in schools." Hoover, AL: National Association of School Resource Officers.

40. Na and Gottfredson (2013).

41. Matthew T. Theriot (2009) "School resource officers and the criminalization of student behavior." *Journal of Criminal Justice* 37: 280–287. Note, though, that Theriot does find reductions in arrests for assault and weapons charges.

42. Kerrin C. Wolf (2013) "Booking students: An analysis of school arrests and court outcomes." *Northwestern Journal of Law and Social Policy* 9: 58–87; see also Udi Ofer, Angela Jones, Johanna Miller, Deinya Phenix, Tara Bahl, Christina Mokhtar, and Chase Madar (2009) "Safety with dignity: Alternatives to the over-policing of schools." New York, NY: New York Civil Liberties Union (p. 10).

43. Michael P. Krezmien, Peter E. Leone, Mark S. Zablocki, and Craig S. Wells (2010) "Juvenile court referrals and the public schools: Nature and extent of the practice in five states." *Journal of Contemporary Criminal Justice* 26: 273–293.

44. Jason P. Nance (in press) "Students, police, and the school-to-prison pipeline." *Washington University Law Review*.

45. Judge Steven C. Teske and Judge J. Brian Huff (2011) "When did making adults mad become a crime? The court's role in dismantling the school-to-prison pipeline." *Juvenile and Family Justice Today* (Winter): 14–17. Accessed online at www.ncjfcj.org/sites/default/files/Today%20Winter%202011Feature%20 %282%29.pdf.

46. Teske and Huff (2011).

47. See George Sugai and Robert Horner (2002) "The evolution of discipline practices: School-wide positive behavior supports." *Child and Family Behavior Therapy* 24: 23–50.

48. See Morgan et al. (2014).

49. As of September 10, 2015; see www.ojjdp.gov/mpg/Topic/Details/94.

50. Ofer et al. (2009).

CHAPTER 3. EXTENDING INEQUALITY

1. From President Obama's "Back to School Speech" (as prepared for delivery) given to students in Philadelphia on September 14, 2010. Accessed online at www.whitehouse.gov/the-press-office/2010/09/13/remarks-president-barack-obama-prepared-delivery-back-school-speech.

2. For example, Prudence Carter (2007) *Keepin' It Real: School Success beyond Black and White.* New York, NY: Oxford University Press; Jonathan Kozol (2012) *Savage Inequalities: Children in America's Schools.* New York, NY: Broadway

Books; Annette Lareau (2011) *Unequal Childhoods: Class, Race and Family Life, 2nd ed.* Berkeley, CA: University of California Press; Pedro A. Noguera (2003) *City Schools and the American Dream: Reclaiming the Promise of Public Education.* New York, NY: Teachers College Press.

3. For example, Jeannie Oakes (1985) *Keeping Track: How Schools Structure Inequality.* New Haven, CT: Yale University Press; Jonathan Kozol (2005) *The Shame of the Nation: The Restoration of Apartheid Schooling in America.* New York, NY: Random House.

4. Pierre Bourdieu (translated by Richard Nice) (1984) *Distinction: A Social Critique of the Judgement of Taste.* Cambridge, MA: Harvard University Press.

5. Pierre Bourdieu and Jean-Claude Passeron (translated by Richard Nice) (1990) *Reproduction in Education, Society and Culture, 2nd ed.* Thousand Oaks, CA: Sage; Lareau (2011).

6. Fine et al. (2004); Nolan (2011); Rios (2011).

7. See Irwin et al. (2013); Kupchik and Ward (2014); Jason P. Nance (2013) "Students, security and race." *Emory Law Journal* 63: 1–57; Payne and Welch (2010); Welch and Payne (2010, 2012).

8. Rocque and Paternoster (2011); Russell J. Skiba, Choong-Geun Chung, Megan Trachok, Timberly L. Baker, Adam Sheya, and Robin L. Hughes (2014) "Parsing disciplinary disproportionality: Contributions of infraction, student, and school characteristics to out-of-school suspension and expulsion." *American Educational Research Journal* 51: 540–670; Shi-Chang Wu, William Pink, Robert Crain, and Oliver Moles (1982) "Student suspension: A critical reappraisal." *Urban Review* 14: 245–303.

9. U.S. Department of Education, Office of Civil Rights (2014) "Civil Rights Data Collection: Data Snapshot (School Discipline)." Accessed online at www2.ed.gov/about/offices/list/ocr/docs/crdc-discipline-snapshot.pdf.

10. Payne and Welch (2010); Welch and Payne (2010, 2012); see also Irwin et al. (2013); Nance (2013).

11. Rocque and Paternoster (2011).

12. Irwin et al. (2013).

13. David M. Ramey (2015) "The social structure of criminalized and medicalized school discipline." *Sociology of Education* 88: 181–201.

14. Kupchik and Ward (2014).

15. Jacquelyn Byers, Jasmine Jones, Micha Cornelius, Jory Steele, Christopher Bridges, Laura Faer, and Sarah Omojola (2013) "From report card to criminal record: The impact of policing Oakland youth." Oakland, CA: Black Organizing Project, Public Counsel, and the ACLU of Northern California; New York City School-Justice Partnership Task Force (2013); W. David Stevens, Lauren Sartain, Elaine M. Allenswroth, and Rachel Levenstein (2015) "Discipline practices in Chicago schools: Trends in the use of suspensions and arrests." Chicago, IL: University of Chicago Consortium on Chicago School Research.

16. Anthony A. Peguero and Zahra Shakarkar (2011) "Latino/a student misbehavior and school punishment." *Hispanic Journal of Behavioral Sciences* 33: 54–70. Not only does this study demonstrate greater likelihood of punishment for some Latino/a youth, it also highlights the importance of considering immigration status as well. More recent studies have begun to explore this theme further, finding that school-violence prevention efforts and efforts to integrate immigrant students may actually backfire for immigrant students, putting them and other students at greater risk of violence; see Stephanie M. DiPietro, Lee Ann Slocum, and Finn-Age Esbensen (2015) "School climate and violence: Does immigrant status matter?" *Youth Violence and Juvenile Justice* 13: 299–322; Rachel Garver and Pedro Noguera (2015) "Supported and unsafe: The impact of educational structures for immigrant students on school safety." *Youth Violence and Juvenile Justice* 13: 323–344.

17. For example, John M. Wallace, Sarah Goodkind, Cynthia M. Wallace, and Jerald G. Bachman (2008) "Racial, ethnic, and gender differences in school discipline among U.S. high school students: 1991–2005." *Negro Educational Review* 59: 47–62.

18. For example, Rocque and Paternoster (2011). Finding no difference between Latino/a and other students may be because all Latino/a youths are usually considered to be a single group, without attention to their generational status, despite greater risk of punishment only for third-generation immigrant Latino/a students rather than more recent immigrants. Notably, Ramey (2015) finds that schools with larger populations of Hispanic youths tend to have significantly lower suspension rates than other schools.

19. See also Wallace et al. (2008).

20. Rocque and Paternoster (2011); Skiba et al. (2014); Wu et al. (1982).

21. Kupchik and Ward (2014).

22. Ramey (2015).

23. Rocque and Paternoster (2011); Skiba et al. (2014).

24. See Edward W. Morris (2007) "'Ladies' or 'loudies?' Perceptions and experiences of Black girls in classrooms." *Youth and Society* 38: 490–515.

25. Kathryn E. W. Himmelstein and Hannah Bruckner (2011) "Criminal-justice and school sanctions against nonheterosexual youth: A national longitudinal study." *Pediatrics* 127: 49–57.

26. See also Preston Mitchum and Aisha C. Moodie-Mills (2014) "Beyond bullying: How hostile school climate perpetuates the school-to-prison-pipeline for LGBT youth." Washington, DC: Center for American Progress.

27. See Kim et al. (2010); Rocque and Paternoster (2011).

28. Daniel J. Losen and Jonathan Gillespie (2012) "Opportunities suspended: The disparate impact of disciplinary exclusion from school." Los Angeles, CA: UCLA Civil Rights Project. Accessed online at http://civilrightsproject.ucla.edu /resources/projects/center-for-civil-rights-remedies/school-to-prison-folder

/federal-reports/upcoming-ccrr-research/losen-gillespie-opportunity-suspended-2012.pdf.

29. See Patricia Hill Collins (2000) *Black Feminist Thought: Knowledge, Consciousness, and the Politics of Empowerment, 2nd ed.* New York, NY: Routledge; Kimberlé W. Crenshaw, Neil Gotanda, and Garry Peler (1995) *Critical Race Theory: The Key Writings That Formed the Movement.* New York, NY: New Press. Intersectionality became popular after sociologist Patricia Hill Collins used it to move beyond traditional feminist perspectives, which were based largely on middle-class white women's experiences only. She argued that we need to consider how being a woman can mean different things based on one's race, class, and context.

30. Ferguson (2000).

31. Kimberlé Williams Crenshaw, Pricilla Ocen, and Jyoti Nanda (2015) "Black girls matter: Pushed out, overpoliced and underprotected." New York, NY: Columbia University Center for Intersectionality and Social Policy Studies; Wallace et al. (2008).

32. Morris (2007); see also Crenshaw et al. (2015).

33. Kupchik and Ward (2014).

34. See Danfeng Soto-Vigil Koon (2013) "Exclusionary school discipline: An issue brief and review of the literature." University of California, Berkeley School of Law: Chief Justice Earl Warren Institute on Law and Social Policy.

35. See www.cdc.gov/healthyyouth/data/yrbs/overview.htm.

36. Skiba et al. (2000), p. 6.

37. Carter (2007); Ferguson (2000); Lewis (2003).

38. John J. Brent (2015) "School discipline: Punishing more than bodies." Ph.D. dissertation, University of Delaware.

39. Fabelo et al. (2011).

40. See Ojmarrh Mitchell (2005) "A meta-analysis of race and sentencing research: Explaining the inconsistencies." *Journal of Quantitative Criminology* 21: 439–466.

41. A recent experimental study of teachers' responses to students finds that stereotypes held by teachers about Black youths result in labeling them as troublemakers and in harsher punishments for Black youths who behave similarly to White youths, particularly for repeat minor offenses. See Jason A. Okonufua and Jennifer L. Eberhardt (2015) "Two strikes: Race and the disciplining of young students." *Psychological Science* 26: 617–624.

42. For example, William A. Smith, Man Hung, and Jeremy D. Franklin (2011) "Racial battle fatigue and the miseducation of Black men: Racial microaggressions, societal problems, and environmental stress." *Journal of Negro Education* 80: 63–82.

43. Ferguson (2000); Rios (2011).

44. Focusing only on specific events also directs too much attention to individual officers, rather than to their commanders who train, supervise, and deploy them. This makes it too easy for those who feel oppressed to forget that these officers put themselves in harm's way in an effort to help a community. While individual officers who abuse their authority and act with cruelty must be held accountable, it is vitally important that we consider the broader environment in which they work and how they are instructed to do their jobs.

45. See www.naacp.org/press/entry/naacp-is-deeply-disappointed-a-missouri-grand-jury-opted-not-to-indict-offi.

46. See www.justice.gov/sites/default/files/opa/press-releases/attachments/2015/03/04/ferguson_police_department_report.pdf.

47. See Patrick J. Carr, Laura Napolitano, and Jessica Keating (2007) "We never call the cops and here is why: A qualitative examination of legal cynicism in three Philadelphia neighborhoods." *Criminology* 45: 445–480; Ronald Weitzer and Rod K. Brunson (2009) "Strategic responses to the police among inner-city youth." *Sociological Quarterly* 50: 235–256.

48. See Rios (2011); Shedd (2015).

CHAPTER 4. HURTING FAMILIES

1. For example, Kayla Cripps and Brett Zyromski (2009) "Adolescents' psychological well-being and perceived parental involvement: Implications for parental involvement in middle schools." *AMLE Online: Research in Middle Level Education* 33: 1–14; Nurit Kaplan Toren (2013) "Multiple dimensions of parental involvement and its links to young adolescent self-evaluation and academic achievement." *Psychology in the Schools* 50: 634–649; David L. Williams and Nancy Feyl Chavkin (1989) "Essential elements of strong parent involvement programs." *Educational Leadership* 47: 18–20; Michigan Department of Education (2002) "What research says about parent involvement in children's education." Accessed online at www.dupage.k12.il.us/_includes/services/pdf/Final_Parent_Involvement_Fact_Sheet_14732_7.pdf.

CHAPTER 5. HOW SCHOOLS TEACH BULLYING

1. Dan Olweus (1993) *Bullying at School: What We Know and What We Can Do.* Oxford: Blackwell.

2. See Ronnie Casella (2001) *"Being Down": Challenging Violence in Urban Schools.* New York, NY: Teachers College Press; Michel Fine (1991) *Framing Dropouts: Notes on the Politics of an Urban High School.* Albany, NY: SUNY Press; Nolan (2011).

3. John H. Hoover and Ronald L. Oliver (2008) *The Bullying Prevention Handbook: A Guide for Principals, Teachers, and Counselors, 2nd ed.* Bloomington, IN: Solution Tree; Tonja R. Nansel, Mary D. Overpeck, Denise L. Haynie, W. June Ruan, and Peter C. Scheidt (2003) "Relationships between bullying and violence among U.S. youth." *Archives of Pediatric Adolescent Medicine* 157: 348–353.

4. Brent J. Litwiller and Amy M. Brausch (2013) "Cyber bullying and physical bullying in adolescent suicide: The role of violent behavior and substance use." *Journal of Youth and Adolescence* 42: 675–684.

5. Catherine P. Bradshaw, Tracy Evian Waasdorp, Asha Goldweber, and Sarah Lindstron Johnson (2013) "Bullies, gangs, drugs, and school: Understanding the overlap and the role of ethnicity and urbanicity." *Journal of Youth and Adolescence* 42: 220–234; Olweus (1993).

6. Meda Chesney-Lind and Katherine Irwin (2007) *Beyond Bad Girls: Gender, Violence and Hype.* New York, NY: Routledge.

7. Dena T. Sacco, Katharine Silbaugh, Felipe Corredor, June Casey, and Davis Doherty (2012) "An overview of state anti-bullying legislation and other related laws." Accessed online at http://cyber.law.harvard.edu/sites/cyber.law.harvard.edu/files/State_Anti_bullying_Legislation_Overview_0.pdf.

8. See www.violencepreventionworks.org/public/index.page.

9. Denise L. Haynie, Tonja Nansel, Patricia Eitel, Aria David Crump, Keith Saylor, Kai Yu, and Bruce Simon-Morton (2001) "Bullies, victims, and bully/victims: Distinct groups of at-risk youth." *Journal of Early Adolescence* 21: 29–49.

10. For example, Christopher Bagley, Michael Wood, and Loretta Young (1994) "Victim to abuser: Mental health and behavioral sequels of child sexual abuse in a community survey of young adult males." *Child Abuse & Neglect* 18: 683–697; Angela Browne and David Finkelhor (1986) "Impact of child sexual abuse: A review of the research." *Psychological Bulletin* 99: 66–77.

11. On smoking, see Christine Jackson and Lisa Henriksen (1997) "Do as I say: Parent smoking, antismoking socialization, and smoking onset among children." *Addictive Behaviors* 22: 107–114; on drinking, see Mark W. Roosa, Irwin N. Sandler, Janette Beals, and Jerome L. Short (1988) "Risk status of adolescent children of problem-drinking parents." *American Journal of Community Psychology* 16: 225–269; on voting, see David E. Campbell (2006) *Why We Vote: How Schools and Communities Shape Our Civic Life.* Princeton, NJ: Princeton University Press.

12. Additional details about this dataset, our analyses, and our results can be found in Aaron Kupchik and Katie A. Farina (2016) "Imitating authority: Students' perceptions of school punishment and security, and bullying victimization." *Youth Violence and Juvenile Justice* 14: 147–163.

13. Julie Gerlinger and James C. Wo (in press) "Preventing school bullying: Should schools prioritize an authoritative school discipline approach over security measures?" *Journal of School Violence.*

CHAPTER 6. CIVIC PARTICIPATION IN THE FUTURE

1. U.S. Department of Education (2012) Digest of Education Statistics, table 40. Accessed online at http://nces.ed.gov/programs/digest/d12/tables/dt12_040 .asp.

2. See http://school.familyeducation.com/home-schooling/decision-making /39267.html?page = 2&detoured = 1.

3. Caccamo is quoted by Patrick Cohn (2009) "Five benefits for kids who participate in sports." Accessed online at www.youthsportspsychology.com /youth_sports_psychology_blog/?p = 213.

4. David Tyack (1974) *The One Best System: A History of American Urban Education*. Cambridge, MA: Harvard University Press. See also Stanley William Rothstein (1984) *The Power to Punish: A Social Inquiry into Coercion and Control in Urban Schools*. New York, NY: University Press of America; Robert H. Wiebe (1967) *The Search for Order: 1877–1920*. New York, NY: Hill and Wang.

5. See Samuel Bowles and Herbert Gintis (1977) *Schooling in Capitalist America: Educational Reform and the Contradictions of Economic Life*. New York, NY: Basic Books.

6. While the division between workers is less clear in today's labor market, clear distinctions between the education of wealthy and poor students help maintain class inequality; see, for example, Kozol (2005).

7. For example, Myra Sadker and David Sadker (1995) *Failing at Fairness: How Our Schools Cheat Girls*. New York, NY: Touchstone; David Beede, Tiffany Julian, David Langdon, George McKittrick, Beethika Khan, and Mark Doms (2011) "Women in STEM: A Gender Gap to Innovation, Executive Summary." Issue Brief 04–11. Washington, DC: U.S. Department of Commerce, Economics and Statistics Administration.

8. For example, Michael W. Apple and James A. Beane (1999) *Democratic Schools: Lessons from the Chalk Face*. Buckingham, UK: Open University Press.

9. Robert D. Putnam (2001) *Bowling Alone: The Collapse and Revival of American Community*. New York, NY: Simon and Schuster.

10. For example, Campbell (2006).

11. Apple and Beane (1999).

12. For example, Fabelo et al. (2011).

13. See also Fine et al. (2004).

14. Aaron Sussman (2012) "Learning in lockdown: School police, race, and the limits of law." *UCLA Law Review* 59: 788–849 (see p. 826). Note that the first method of denying civic opportunity that Sussman refers to is to funnel students into the justice system.

15. Sentencing Project (2014) "Fact sheet: Felony disenfranchisement laws." Washington, DC: Sentencing Project. Accessed online at http://sentencingproject .org/doc/publications/fd_Felony%20Disenfranchisement%20Laws%20in%20

the%20US.pdf; see also Alexander (2010); Jeff Manza and Chris Uggen (2008) *Locked Out: Felon Disenfranchisement and American Democracy.* New York, NY: Oxford University Press.

16. Surbhi Godsay, Kei Kawashima-Ginsberg, Abby Kiesa, and Peter Levine (2012) "'That's not democracy': How out-of-school youth engage in civic life and what stands in their way." Medford, MA: CIRCLE/Kettering Foundation (see p. 38).

17. For example, Jeffrey Fagan and Tom R. Tyler (2005) "Legal socialization of children and adolescents." *Social Justice Research* 18: 217–242; David S. Kirk and Mauri Matsuda (2011) "Legal cynicism, collective efficacy, and the ecology of arrest." *Criminology* 49: 443–472.

18. See Aaron Kupchik and Thomas Catlaw (2015) "Discipline and participation: The long-term effects of suspension and school security on the political and civic engagement of youth." *Youth & Society* 47: 95–124.

19. See Fabelo et al. (2011); Kupchik (2010).

CHAPTER 7. FINANCIAL COSTS OF SCHOOL SECURITY AND PUNISHMENT

1. Robers et al. (2015): table 20.3.

2. Robers et al. (2015): table 20.2.

3. This is an approximate figure reflecting September 2013 enrollment, rounded to preserve the district's anonymity, based on information from the district's website.

4. See Digest of Education Statistics: table 216.40. Accessed online at http://nces.ed.gov/programs/digest/d13/tables/dt13_216.40.asp.

5. *Red Clay Record,* December 2014, p. 2 (Red Clay Consolidated School District, Delaware).

6. Kupchik and Ward (2014).

7. Kozol (2012).

8. Title 14, 701, Unit Count. Accessed online at http://regulations.delaware.gov/AdminCode/title14/700/701.pdf.

9. Morgan et al. (2014), p. 10. For documentation of San Antonio losses, the report cites Kathryn Freeman et al. (2012) "Breaking rules, breaking budgets: Cost of exclusionary discipline in 11 Texas school districts." Austin, TX: Texas Appleseed. For documentation of Fresno losses, the report cites Children Now (2013) "Restorative justice practices: How Fresno Unified School District can boost student attendance, improve graduation rates, and increase funding." Oakland, CA: Children Now.

10. Fabelo et al. (2011).

11. Miner P. Marchbanks III, Jamilia J. Blake, Eric A. Booth, Dottie Carmichael, Allison L. Seibert, and Tony Fabelo (2013) "The economic effects of exclusionary discipline on grade retention and high school dropout." Center for Civil Rights Remedies and the Research-to-Practice Collaborative, National Conference, January 2013.

12. Marchbanks et al. (2013), p. 17.

13. They rely considerably on prior analyses in Roman Alvarez et al. (2009) "The ABCD's of Texas education: Assessing the benefits and costs of reducing the dropout rate." College Station, TX: Bush School of Government and Public Service, Texas A&M University.

14. Marchbanks et al. (2013), p. 18

15. Robert Balfanz, Vaughan Byrnes, and Joanna Fox (2013) "Sent home and put off-track: The antecedents, disproportionalities, and consequences of being suspended in the ninth grade." Center for Civil Rights Remedies and the Research-to-Practice Collaborative, National Conference, January 2013.

16. Talisha Lee, Dewey Cornell, Anne Gregory, and Xitao Fan (2011) "High suspension schools and dropout rates for Black and White students." *Education & Treatment of Children* 34: 167–192.

17. This is the figure calculated by Alvarez et al. (2009) and used by Marchbanks et al. (2013).

18. Based on U.S. Census Bureau, "Current Population Survey: Median household income (in 2013 inflation-adjusted dollars) by state ranked from highest to lowest using 3-year average: 2011–2013." Accessed online at www.census.gov/hhes/www/income/data/statemedian/.

19. Texas's state and local payments per capita are $434.30, compared to $750.50 for all states combined, according to data found at www.usgovernment spending.com/compare_state_welfare_spend.

20. Alliance for Excellent Education (2011) "The high cost of high school dropouts: What the nation pays for inadequate high schools." Issue Brief, November.

21. Justice Policy Institute (2009) "The costs of confinement: Why good juvenile justice policies make good fiscal sense." Washington, DC: Justice Policy Institute.

22. See table "National estimates of juvenile court processing for delinquency cases, all cases." Accessed online at http://ojjdp.gov/ojstatbb/ezajcs/asp/process .asp.

23. See Melissa Sickmund et al. (2013) "Easy access to the Census of Juveniles in Residential Placement." Accessed online at www.ojjdp.gov/ojstatbb/ezacjrp/.

24. See Aaron Kupchik (2006) *Judging Juveniles: Prosecuting Adolescents in Adult and Juvenile Courts.* New York, NY: NYU Press.

25. Fabelo et al. (2011), p. 72.

26. As stated above, Sickmund et al. (2013) report that the most common length of custodial placement is 91–180 days; here I use the midpoint, 135 days.

27. See Annie E. Casey Foundation (2013) "Youth incarceration in the United States." Accessed online at www.aecf.org/m/resourcedoc/aecf-Youth IncarcerationInfographic-2013.pdf.

28. Na and Gottfredson (2013), p. 635.

29. See Kupchik (2010).

30. All court statistics are from Melissa Sickmund et al. (2014) "Easy access to juvenile court statistics: 1985–2011." Accessed online at www.ojjdp.gov/ojstatbb /ezajcs/.

31. In 1985 there were 6,400 youths placed in correctional facilities for simple assault; in 2011 there were 12,600. See www.ojjdp.gov/ojstatbb/ezajcs/asp/process .asp.

32. Babcock (2009).

33. See David S. Kirk and Robert J. Sampson (2013) "Juvenile arrest and collateral educational damage in the transition to adulthood." *Sociology of Education* 86: 36–62; Gary Sweeten (2006) "Who will graduate? Disruption of high school education by arrest and court involvement." *Justice Quarterly* 23: 462–480.

34. Rios (2011).

35. Kupchik and Ward (2014); Payne and Welch (2010); Welch and Payne (2010, 2012).

36. See Ronnie Casella (2006) *Selling Us the Fortress: The Promotion of Techno-Security Equipment for Schools*. New York, NY: Routledge.

8. CONCLUSION

1. For example, Lareau (2011).

2. See http://abcnews.go.com/GMA/be_your_best/page/top-10-stressful-jobs-america-14355387.

3. Jeffrey M. Jones (2012) "Confidence in U.S. public schools at new low." *Gallup*, June 20. Accessed online at www.gallup.com/poll/155258/Confidence-Public-Schools-New-Low.aspx.

4. Tamar Lewin (2010) "School chief dismisses 241 teachers in Washington." *The New York Times*, July 23. Accessed online at www.nytimes.com/2010/07/24 /education/24teachers.html?_r = 0.

5. Jennifer Medina (2014) "Judge rejects teacher tenure for California." *The New York Times*, June 10. Accessed online at www.nytimes.com/2014/06/11/us /california-teacher-tenure-laws-ruled-unconstitutional.html.

6. For example, Karen Sternheimer (2006) *Kids These Days: Facts and Fictions about Today's Youth*. New York, NY: Rowman and Littlefield.

7. See Arum (2003); Grant (1990); Paul Sperry (2015) "How liberal discipline policies are making schools less safe." *New York Post*, March 14. Accessed online

at http://nypost.com/2015/03/14/politicians-are-making-schools-less-safe-and-ruining-education-for-everyone/.

APPENDIX

1. For additional details, see Kupchik and Farina (2016).
2. For additional details, see Kupchik and Catlaw (2015).
3. This research uses data from Add Health, a program project designed by J. Richard Udry, Peter S. Bearman, and Kathleen Mullan Harris and funded by grant P01-HD31921 from the Eunice Kennedy Shriver National Institute of Child Health and Human Development, with cooperative funding from seventeen other agencies. Special acknowledgment is due to Ronald R. Rindfuss and Barbara Entwisle for assistance in the original design. Persons interested in obtaining data files from Add Health should contact Add Health, The University of North Carolina at Chapel Hill, Carolina Population Center, 123 W. Franklin Street, Chapel Hill, NC 27516–2524 (addhealth@unc.edu). No direct support was received from grant P01-HD31921 for this analysis.

Index